catching
readers

THE RESEARCH-INFORMED CLASSROOM SERIES

Consider daily life for a child struggling with reading. Imagine what it is like to go through school day after day feeling that you are bad at the one thing that school seems to value most. Imagine struggling with everything from independent reading to reading directions on a math worksheet. Imagine what that feels like. . . .

While there are all sorts of pressures to improve instruction for struggling readers—to raise test scores, to make adequate yearly progress (AYP), and so on—the most compelling reason is to help as many children as possible avoid that feeling. We want to enable children to go through elementary school feeling, and being, successful.

Barbara Taylor brings decades of research and development to the question of how to help struggling readers become successful. *Catching Readers: Grade 1*, which is part of the Early Intervention in Reading series, brings the resulting insights to you, in the form of concrete and specific practices that have been shown to help children who struggle improve their reading. These books could not come at a more important time, as response to intervention (RTI) leads schools to invest more than ever in small-group reading instruction. The multifaceted and responsive teaching at the heart of the approach Taylor describes is a welcome contrast to the myopic, scripted programs marketed so heavily under the banner of RTI.

These books exemplify the ideals of the Research-Informed Classroom series—bringing rigorous classroom-based research to bear on persistent challenges of classroom practice. This series aims to bridge the gap between research and practice by focusing on the most practical, classroom-relevant research and communicating practices based on that research in a way that makes them accessible, appealing, and actionable. The series is founded on the belief that students and teachers are researchers' clients, and serving them should be the highest priority.

As with so much of the best educational research and development, Taylor has collaborated extensively with teachers close to home and throughout the United States. Indeed, one might say we've gone full circle, from Teacher-Informed Research to Research-Informed Teaching. So thank you, teachers, and thank you, Barbara, for this important contribution to reading success for all children.

—*Nell K. Duke*

MICHIGAN STATE UNIVERSITY

catching
readers

grade 1

DAY-BY-DAY SMALL-GROUP READING INTERVENTIONS

Barbara M. Taylor

HEINEMANN
Portsmouth, NH

KH

Heinemann
361 Hanover Street
Portsmouth, NH 03801–3912
www.heinemann.com

Offices and agents throughout the world

The author and publisher wish to thank those who have generously given permission to reprint borrowed material in this book and/or on the DVD:

Cover art and excerpt from *Geraldine's Blanket* by Holly Keller. Copyright © 1984 by Holly Keller. Used by permission of HarperCollins Publishers.

Cover and interior art from *Rosie's Walk* by Pat Hutchins. Copyright © 1968 by Patricia Hutchins. Published by Simon & Schuster Books for Young Readers, an imprint of Simon & Schuster Children's Publishing Division. Used by permission of the publisher.

Cover and interior art from *Kit and Kat* by Tomie dePaola. Copyright © 1986 by the Philip Lief Group, copyright © 1994 by Grosset & Dunlap, Inc. Used by permission of Grosset & Dunlap, a Division of Penguin Young Readers Group, a Member of Penguin Group (USA) Inc., 345 Hudson Street, New York, NY 10014. All rights reserved.

Table 4-1: "Characteristics of Grade 1 Books at Different EIR Levels" from *Guided Reading: Good First Teaching for All Children* by Irene C. Fountas and Gay Su Pinnell. Copyright © 1996 by Irene C. Fountas and Gay Su Pinnell. Published by Heinemann, Portsmouth, NH. All rights reserved.

Library of Congress Cataloging-in-Publication Data

Taylor, Barbara M.
    Catching readers, grade 1 : day-by-day small-group reading interventions / Barbara M. Taylor.
       p. cm.—(Early intervention in reading series) (The research-informed classroom series)
    Includes bibliographical references.
    ISBN-13: 978-0-325-02888-0
    ISBN-10: 0-325-02888-5
    1. Reading—Remedial teaching. 2. Individualized instruction. I. Title. II. Title: Catching readers, grade one.
    LB1050.5.T33 2010
    372.43—dc22
                           2010006727

Editor: Wendy Murray
Production editor: Patricia Adams
Video editor: Sherry Day
Video producer: Bob Schuster, Real Productions
Cover design: Lisa Fowler
Typesetter: Gina Poirier Design
Manufacturing: Valerie Cooper

Printed in the United States of America on acid-free paper
14 13 12 11 10 ML 1 2 3 4 5

4/15/13

This book is dedicated to the many first-grade teachers who work tirelessly to provide motivating instruction that meets their students' needs, challenges them all, and is instrumental to their success in reading.

Contents

1 Helping First Graders Who Struggle
Lessons That Sit Within Effective Reading Instruction **1**

2 Meet the Teachers
The Differentiated Lessons and Teacher
Collaboration That Support EIR **19**

3 The Three-Day Lesson Routine **32**

8 Creating an EIR Community   **114**

On the DVD

See-It-in-Action Video Clips

Day 1 Lesson:

Day 2 Lesson:

Day 3 Lesson:

 Downloadable Classroom Reproducibles
Over 100 pages of full-size forms and teaching resources.

Teaching Resources on the DVD

Chapter 4

Chapter 5

Chapter 6

Chapter 7

Chapter 8

Foreword

● ●

I began my teaching career as a first-grade teacher in Key West, Florida, in 1965. Much has changed since then in the world and in the world of school. But reading Barbara Taylor's books made me realize how much is still the same. My class of thirty-five children contained nine children—two girls and seven boys—who were (in the lingo of the day) "not ready." In those days, basal reading series for first grade had a readiness book that I was very grateful to find. I grouped these nine students together and we made our way through the workbook pages. The pages were mostly practice with letter names and auditory discrimination—the precursor of phonemic awareness. Six weeks into the school year, we finished the readiness book and I administered the Metropolitan Readiness Test to my students. For three days, I tried to keep them focused on the correct lines and asked them to underline the letter *b*, put an *x* on the picture that began like *paint*, and circle the picture of the object that rhymed with *cat*. I took all these booklets home and spent a miserable weekend grading them. As I made my way through the test booklets, I adopted a "benefit of the doubt" scoring system. "Two red marks on this line, none on the next. If the second mark is on the next line, it would be right. I'm counting it correct." In spite of my lenient scoring, scores for eight of the nine children indicated they were still "not ready." I spent a sleepless Sunday night wondering what I was to do with these children who were clearly not ready when I had used up all the readiness materials! Lacking any alternative, I started them in the first pre-primer and we plodded our way through the books. By the end of the year, only one of these students could read fluently at primer level.

If Barbara had written her books 45 years earlier (when she was probably in kindergarten), I think I could have transformed my "not ready" kids into fluent readers. Based on many years of research in real classrooms with real teachers and kids, Barbara has created a workable system for providing struggling readers in grades K–5 with the targeted intervention they need to become fluent readers. At the heart of Early Intervention in Reading (EIR) is the addition of a second reading lesson in a small-group setting. Unlike many interventions, struggling readers get this second reading lesson *in addition to* all the rich classroom instruction and *in* the classroom—not in some room down the hall. With details, specifics, and examples that only someone who has spent many hours in the classroom could know, Barbara guides you step-by-step as you organize for and provide effective EIR instruction. As you read through the book, your brain races with questions:

▶ "How do I fit an additional intervention group lesson into my daily schedule?"

▶ "What books work best for these lessons?"

▶ "How can I provide all the instruction struggling readers need in 20 minutes?"

- ▶ "What does the coaching for decoding and comprehension look like and sound like?"

- ▶ "How do I wean them off my coaching and move them toward independence?"

- ▶ "How do I provide worthwhile independent activities for the students I am not working with?"

Because Barbara has worked in many so classrooms coaching teachers who are implementing EIR, she can provide practical, classroom-tested answers to all your questions. She invites you into the classrooms of real teachers and you get to hear them describing how they organize and problem solve. In addition to the printed resource, you can go to the video clips on the DVD to "See It in Action." As you watch real teachers move through the three-day lesson sequence, you realize that, while it is complex, Barbara provides all the resources you need to make it work in your classrooms with your students who struggle.

Once you see how EIR works in your classroom, you will probably want to spread the word. Not to worry! Barbara is right there supporting you. In the final chapter, "Creating an EIR Community," she provides a detailed, month-by-month plan for organizing a group of colleagues to learn together how to better meet the needs of struggling readers.

So, if they ever invent a time machine that could transport me back to 1965, with the help of Barbara Taylor's books, I know I could teach all my "not ready" kids to read!

Patricia M. Cunningham
Wake Forest University

Acknowledgments

This book is the result of twenty years of collaboration with many first-grade teachers and colleagues across the United States. I want to thank them all for their invaluable contributions to this book.

Inspired by Reading Recovery, I developed the Early Intervention in Reading (EIR) process in the late 1980s to help first-grade teachers help their at-risk readers succeed in reading through daily, small-group intervention lessons. I have refined the EIR process over the years by visiting many classrooms and working with and learning from many teachers and their students. Without this opportunity, I would not have been able to modify and improve the EIR teaching strategies and professional learning practices described in this book.

I also want to thank the hundreds of first-grade teachers I have visited and learned from over the past ten years through my work on effective reading instruction and school-wide reading improvement. I especially want to thank the exemplary teachers who have contributed so much to this book by sharing their thoughts and effective reading lessons.

I owe a special thanks and a debt of gratitude to my colleague, Ceil Critchley, a master teacher who has helped teachers succeed with EIR through the phenomenal professional learning support she has provided to them over many years. Without Ceil's expert guidance, teachers would not have been as successful as they have been in helping their at-risk readers learn to read well by the end of first grade.

I also want to recognize my academic colleagues for their support and feedback. In particular, thanks to my good friends, Kathy Au and Taffy Raphael, for gently nudging me over the years to publish my work on EIR in a form readily accessible to teachers.

I want to thank the many people at Heinemann who have made this book possible. First, thanks to Wendy Murray, my editor, who saw the value of this book for teachers with its focus on an instructional process, not materials and a script to follow, for at-risk readers. She has done a remarkable job cutting unnecessary chunks, adding teacher-friendly phrases, reorganizing entire sections, and designing the book so it is easy for teachers to read and use. I also want to thank Patty Adams, my production editor, for her top-notch work on a complex project within a challenging time frame. Whenever I called with questions or concerns, she responded cheerfully and promptly. Many others at Heinemann have also contributed to this book and I thank them for their efforts.

It is my sincere hope that first-grade teachers will find this book useful as they strive to teach students who are a little behind in the fall to be confident, successful, readers by the end of the school year. Thanks to all first-grade teachers for the important work you do for our children!

Barbara M. Taylor
University of Minnesota

Introduction

W
e are a culture of quick fixes. We promise mastery in ten easy lessons, instant success, overnight sensations. Go to a bookstore and whether you stand and gaze at the brightly colored covers in the business, health, or education section, the answer to our every need is couched in words like *speedy, easy,* and *seven easy steps.*

In such a culture, a lot of alarm bells go off when a teacher faces e a six-year-old child in first grade who is behind in learning to read. *Catching Readers, Grade 1,* is one book in a series of five. This book is dedicated to giving the regular classroom teacher what's needed to reach and teach that six-year-old. Early Intervention in Reading is a concrete plan rather than a frantic pull-out program or a misguided label. Each book in the series offers teacher-friendly, research-proven background and lessons for young readers who need an extra boost.

The intervention model brings reading success to children in a three-day lesson cycle, which I know sounds as though I'm playing into the same glib promises of swift solutions. I state it here as a way to express that it is a three-day format used across a school year and with deep roots—more than twenty years of classroom testing. I emphasize the "three-day" repetition of the lessons to make it clear that we don't have to choose to run around in circles looking for some new complicated program for reaching at-risk readers. We know what to do. When we're true to children's developmental levels, know which books to put in their hands and provide effective instruction, a lot of good things fall into place. The key is to focus on the children and the practices we know help them to read at each grade level.

In fact, the intervention model I offer stands in opposition to approaches and programs that think the answer to helping K–5 below-grade-level readers achieve is to provide remediation. Above-grade-level, on-grade-level, and below-grade-level readers all need the same thing: sound teaching techniques and developmentally appropriate practices that meet their needs and provide intellectual challenge to all.

Here's an overview of how the interventions are unique and yet similar for each grade level, so you can see the developmentally based, purposeful overlap in the series. The intervention gives teachers, staff developers, principals, and reading coaches a predictable model so that schoolwide coherence is easier to attain. All grade-level models stress word recognition proficiency, high-level comprehension, vocabulary development, and strategic reading. Unique components of the various grade-specific models are described below:

Kindergarten

The daily 10-minute supplemental lessons for kindergarten focus on developing all children's oral language, phonemic awareness, and emergent literacy abilities through literature-based activities. The goal is for all students to leave kindergarten with the skills they need to learn to read in first grade. The more capable children, as they respond to the various activities in EIR lessons, serve as models for the children who are less skilled in oral language and emergent literacy abilities. Less-skilled children who need more support return to some of the story discussion questions and phonemic awareness/emergent literacy activities for an additional 10 minutes a day.

First Grade

First-grade children who start the school year with lower-than-average phonemic awareness abilities and letter–sound knowledge will benefit from EIR lessons. The teacher focuses on accelerating students' literacy learning by deliberately coaching them to use strategies to decode words as they are reading, to actively engage in word work, and to think at a higher level about the meaning of the texts they are reading.

Second Grade

Second-grade readers who can't read a book at a first-grade level at the start of second grade will benefit from the basic EIR routine. The intervention begins with first-grade books and routines of the grade 1 EIR model and then moves into second-grade books a few months later. There is also an accelerated grade 2 routine designed for students who come to second grade as independent readers but who will need additional support to be reading on grade level by the end of the school year.

Third Grade

The grade 3 EIR routine is for children who are reading below grade level when they enter third grade. In the grade 3 EIR model, the focus is on refining students' decoding of multisyllabic words, improving their fluency, developing their vocabulary, and enhancing their comprehension of narrative and informational texts. Ideally, the grade 3 EIR model is done within the context of a cross-age tutoring program in which the third-grade students read to and also tutor first-grade EIR students. The third graders are working on their reading for more than "catching up because they are behind." They look forward to and enjoy working with their younger student who needs additional support in reading.

Fourth/Fifth

The EIR routine for fourth and fifth grade is for children who are reading below grade level at the beginning of the school year. Although students receive support in attacking multisyllabic words and developing reading fluency, the grade 4/5 model focuses on improving students' comprehension of informational text through the use of comprehension strategies, discussion of vocabulary, and engagement in high-level talk and writing about texts. Ideally, the grade 4/5 EIR model is done within the context of a motivating cross-age tutoring program in which fourth and fifth graders read to and also tutor second or third-graders.

Getting Good at It: Different Ways to Use This Book

This book—and by extension all the books in this series—is designed to be used by the individual teacher, a pair or group of teachers, or as part of a schoolwide professional development plan. Here are components that support collaborative learning:

Video Clips for Individual Viewing

As you read about the recurring cycle of EIR routines, I encourage you to watch the video clips that illustrate what is being covered in the text. Many teachers have told me that seeing the EIR routines being applied in the classroom makes it easy to start teaching the EIR lessons. See this icon throughout the book for easy access to the video clips on the DVD.

Guidance for Monthly Sessions with Colleagues

In the last chapter, "Creating an EIR Community," I share a model for a professional learning community (PLC) that works. Over my many years of working with teachers on effective reading instruction generally, and EIR lessons specifically, I have learned from teachers' comments that the collaborative nature of learning new instructional techniques with colleagues leads to excellent understanding, reflection, and success.

Website Support

For additional support, go to www.Heinemann.com and search by Taylor or the title *Catching Readers* for answers to questions that will likely arise about teaching EIR lessons. Also, see the Heinemann website to learn more about the availability of additional support from an EIR expert and consulting support.

We can help so many children become successful readers when we offer excellent reading instruction and provide effective interventions to those students who require additional reading support within their classroom setting. I am excited to have the opportunity to offer my *Catching Readers* series of books to you. Thank you for the important work you do for our children!

catching
readers

Helping First Graders Who Struggle

Lessons That Sit Within Effective Reading Instruction

irst grade in children's literacy lives is a remarkable year. Grade one teachers begin in the fall with a dramatic range of students, from the child who only knows a few letters of the alphabet to the child who walks in on the first day of school and begins to read *The Tale of Despereaux* (DiCamillo 2003) from your classroom book collection. It takes years for teachers to hone their expertise to meet the needs of each child and get them reading to their fullest potential within the momentous first-grade year. This book and the companion video clips and teacher resources on the DVD are aimed at helping teachers arrive at this level of effectiveness sooner.

My career as a researcher and teacher educator has been dedicated to studying and describing components of effective literacy instruction so that teachers can become more intentional in their teaching and more confident in their interactions with children around all aspects of reading instruction. Through this book, my goal is for you to gain a comfort level teaching small-group reading lessons for young children who struggle a bit with reading, but I also aim to show how this intervention work connects to and informs all the rich literacy practices that occur within a balanced literacy framework. In short, when you learn how to teach reading to struggling readers well, I've found it makes you a more effective reading teacher all around.

How the Early Intervention in Reading Model Sits Within Effective Reading Instruction

The small-group intervention lessons featured in this book are based on Early Intervention in Reading (EIR®), a set of teaching practices I developed that incorporates the characteristics of effective reading instruction (see page 3). It's been in practice for twenty years in schools, and if you're a teacher looking to implement Response to Intervention (RTI) or differentiated instruction, you'll see that this model can easily be used to meet these current calls to action.

Early Intervention in Reading provides:

▶ first-grade students struggling to read with an additional daily opportunity to interact with text in a structured, consistent, and comfortable small-group setting

▶ first-grade teachers with a consistent, clear structure that helps them support these children so they can catch up or keep up with grade-level expectations for reading

▶ teachers and schools with an intervention model that isn't stigmatizing for children because it uses authentic literature and instructional practices, and is done within the regular classroom—and usually by the classroom teacher

I want to emphasize that I developed this model with classroom teachers in mind—and it's based on my belief that first graders shouldn't be pulled out of the classroom for extra help. Rather, teachers need to learn to support them during the reading block. They also need to harness the collective power of colleagues and work together to help all children learn to read well.

Through structured, 20-minute lessons, a group of struggling readers are provided with an extra shot of daily quality reading instruction. A regular classroom teacher supports and coaches individual students based on need, so it accelerates students' reading progress. The structure adapts around midyear to children's development as readers, and because it has been refined through decades of research and practice, it's a model that teachers are less likely to abandon or use inconsistently. They see their students making striking gains in their reading, and so it's highly motivating. Later in this chapter and in Chapter 3, we'll look at the three-day lesson cycle in detail, but here is a glimpse of how these lessons extend and amplify the effective reading instruction you do with all your students.

How EIR Meets the Requirements of Effective Reading Instruction

	Effective Reading Instruction	EIR Lessons
What You Teach (Content)	Explicit phonemic awareness instruction	Sound boxes, writing for sounds in sentence writing
	Systematic phonics instruction	Scope and sequence, making words, writing for sounds in sentence writing, coaching in word-recognition strategies
	Oral reading for fluency	Repeated reading of stories, coached reading with feedback, one-on-one reading with aide or volunteer
	Text-based vocabulary instruction	Discussion of word meanings at point of contact in EIR stories
	Comprehension strategies instruction	Summarizing stories, practicing comprehension monitoring
	Comprehension instruction in the context of high-level talk about text	Coaching for high-level comprehension
How You Teach (Pedagogy)	Application of taught skills and strategies to text	Applying taught skills and strategies to text
	Differentiated instruction	Support is provided by teacher to individual students based on need
	Balance of direct teaching and providing support	Coaching students to use taught skills and strategies as they read EIR stories
	Teaching with clear purpose and good timing	Stating teaching purposes routinely, covering daily steps of each 20-minute lesson at a swift pace
	Active student engagement	All students read, write, talk, share with a partner, engage in word work
	Student engagement in challenging, motivating learning activities	Students read stories that require them to "glue to the print" from the beginning, spend only three days on a story, and move on to new challenges with a new text. EIR stories that are selected are engaging texts
	Developing independent learners	High expectations, releasing responsibility to students, partner work
	Motivating classroom community	Using praise, helpful feedback, demonstrating enthusiasm for learning
Professional Learning	Collaborative learning with a focus on practice	Monthly learning meetings to discuss EIR strategies, successes, and challenges

Which Children Need the Intervention and What Is the End Goal?

Students who benefit from EIR lessons are those who come to first grade with relatively weak letter-sound knowledge and phonemic awareness. Without solid intervention lessons, these children are likely to fail to become independent readers in first grade. Early Intervention in Reading strategies were first developed for students in grade 1 (Taylor et al. 1992) and are now developed for students in K–5. The strategies are effective with many different types of regular reading programs (e.g., basal, whole language, reading and writing workshop, systematic phonics). In Chapter 6, I describe the assessments you can use to determine which students might benefit from EIR.

On average, 72 percent of the children who need and receive EIR lessons in first grade are reading independently (on a primer level or higher) by May (Taylor 2001; see this data on the DVD in the research section). It would be wonderful if all students were reading at grade level by May. However, if struggling emergent first-grade readers in May can pick up a book at the primer level that they have never seen before and read it with at least 90 percent accuracy, most will be able to read second-grade material in second grade.

If children can read material sight unseen at the primer level, they understand the alphabetic principle, or the way our reading system works, and they can put this knowledge to work themselves. Follow-up studies demonstrated that 94 percent of the children who were in EIR in first grade were reading on a second-grade level in second grade. In a sub-sample of this group, I found that 89 percent were reading on a third-grade level in third grade.

A Brief Review of the Learning-to-Read Process

Before we turn to the specific model, I want to provide a brief review of the learning-to-read process. To be most effective in helping struggling readers learn how to read, teachers need to have a clear model of what children are learning how to do. Additionally, the elements discussed next tend to be the ones struggling beginning readers have the most trouble internalizing.

The Role of Phonemic Awareness in Learning to Read

Phonemic awareness, or the ability to hear the sounds in words and to blend those sounds together, has been researched extensively. Researchers (Adams 1990; National Reading Panel [NRP] 2000; Snow, Burns, and Griffin 1998) have shown that children who come to first grade with low phonemic awareness are at considerable risk of failing to learn to read in first grade.

Phonemic awareness is one of the two best predictors of reading achievement by the end of first grade. The other predictor is letter-name knowledge. However, quickly teaching children the letter names in first grade does not have a big impact on their May reading achievement because letter-name knowledge serves as a proxy for the literacy environment that children have been in before they get to first grade.

Fortunately, kindergarten interventions, as well as interventions in early first grade, can make a big difference in accelerating children's phonemic awareness and hence impact their reading achievement.

Phonemic awareness is an auditory ability. Segmentation of sounds, blending of sounds, hearing alliteration, and recognizing rhymes are all measures of phonemic awareness. However, the two measures most predictive of end-of-first-grade reading achievement are phoneme segmentation and blending abilities (Adams 1990; NRP 2000; Snow, Burns, and Griffin 1998). For example, a student who gives the sounds in *cat* as /c/ /a/ /t/ is segmenting the sounds. A student who blends the sounds /c/ /a/ /t/ into *cat* is blending sounds into a word.

Partial Decoding and Grasping the Alphabetic Principle

Children begin reading by partially decoding words and using context cues. They typically start using the first letter to sound out a word but cannot get all the way through a word. In fact, beginning readers in first grade sometimes overrely on context to figure out words. The arrows heading downward in Figure 1-1 represents the "aha" moment, or the time at which the lightbulb goes off when children finally understand the alphabetic principle, or how to sound out words. When they get to this point, they understand that within a printed word there are letters that represent phonemes (sounds) that have to be voiced separately and blended together to make up

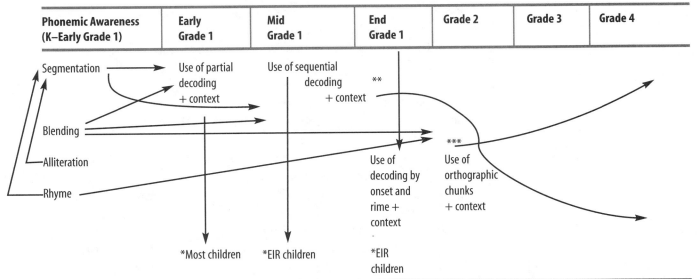

* understands alphabetic principle
** use of context falls off
*** use of automaticity increases

Figure 1-1   Stages of Word Recognition Development

a word. It can be difficult for adults to realize just how challenging this understanding is for children to develop. But many children come to first grade not knowing exactly what makes up a printed word and not knowing what the sounds are in a given word. When you think about it, this is not too surprising because they have never needed to know about the separate sounds in words before.

To adults, the alphabetic principle seems like a simple concept, so we think that if we explain it, children should catch on quickly. Most first-grade children do grasp the alphabetic principle fairly quickly in the fall and then tend to grow very quickly in their reading abilities. Unfortunately, most children who need EIR lessons don't fully grasp the alphabetic principle until January or February and once they do grasp it, they often don't grow quickly in their ability to decode. Some children in EIR—about a third—don't even grasp the alphabetic principle until April or May. This development is just a slower, gradual process for the children who need EIR and something that over the years I have come to accept. As teachers, we need to be patient, believe in the children, and keep working with them. In fact, I am always impressed with the incredible patience demonstrated by the teachers I visit who are using these strategies with their struggling readers.

Learning How to Decode Letter by Letter and by Onset and Rime

Early Intervention in Reading instructional strategies emphasize teaching children to use word-recognition strategies and to depend on themselves as they use these strategies. Letter-by-letter sequential decoding is only one strategy we teach children to use, but it is a very important strategy for them to learn in order to become independent readers. When children come to the word *pig* in their reading, they need to be able to sound out each letter, /p/ /i/ /g/, and blend the sounds together into *pig*. Teachers need to repeatedly model and coach students in letter-by-letter sequential decoding to help them catch on to the alphabetic principle.

Research suggests that children have to understand the concept of letter-by-letter sequential decoding before they can independently decode by onset and rime, or the initial sound and the phonogram that completes the word. (See the Research section on the DVD, "A Brief Review of Research on the Learning-to-Read Process," Taylor 1998, for a review.) Students can decode by onset and rime—/f/ /ind/ is *find*—when prompted to do so. However, they do not regularly use decoding by onset and rime as an independent strategy until they succeed at letter-by-letter sequential decoding.

It is also important to realize that as children start to "glue to the print," or pay attention to the sequence of letters, as they decode words, they begin to rely much less on context to help them figure out words. Teachers need to remind children to think about what would make sense in the story as they are sounding out words because doing so will make it easier for them to come up with the correct word.

By the end of first grade and early into second grade, decoding by onset and rime becomes the preferred decoding strategy for children. That is, if they recognize a chunk (e.g., phonogram) they will decode this way since it is quicker than letter-by-letter sequential decoding (Taylor 1998).

Developing Automaticity

The goal in teaching children to recognize words is that they be able to do so automatically. By second grade and into third grade, children are reading most words automatically as sight words. This doesn't mean that we have to drill on words as sight words; however, through reading for meaning, children develop automaticity for specific words by repeated exposure to these words over time.

By the time children are fully automatic in word recognition, they do not depend on context to help them recognize most words. Of course, there will be words they come across in their reading that they have never seen before, but for the most part, by fourth grade, students typically read with context-free, automatic word recognition.

The Role of Comprehension and Vocabulary in Learning to Read

The purpose of reading is to gain meaning from the text, and it is important to stress both comprehension and vocabulary with emerging readers. Unfortunately, too often, especially with struggling readers, the emphasis on learning to read lies with breaking the code to the neglect of reading for meaning. Effective first-grade teachers, as we see in the lessons of Heather Peterson, John Luther, and Linda Garcia in Chapter 2, emphasize reading for meaning and enjoyment. In EIR lessons, teachers also stress comprehension by including it as one of four steps they cover every day with their struggling readers.

The What and How of Good First-Grade Teaching

EIR was developed with key elements of content (the what) and pedagogy (the how) as its foundation. Effective teachers tend to have a good day-to-day awareness of both content and pedagogy. With that in mind, in Chapter 2 you will meet three teachers—Heather Peterson, John Luther, and Linda Garcia—and you will see what effective teaching looks like in urban, suburban, and rural settings. You'll gain a sense of how these teachers connect EIR lessons to their overall reading instruction. These three teachers not only teach these specialized lessons but provide effective reading instruction to all their students and see excellent growth in their students' reading abilities during each school year.

Content: Four Dimensions Young Children Need

The content of effective reading instruction has many dimensions, all of which develop the abilities students need to become competent readers. These dimensions, listed here, are reinforced with research. They are:

▶ word recognition development (including phonemic awareness and phonics)

▶ fluency development

▶ vocabulary development

▶ comprehension development

Do these elements comprise a complete universe of what leads children to become successful, engaged readers? No, but these are the nonnegotiable aspects of teaching reading in first grade. Without them, all the other practices—from reading aloud picture books to independent reading—won't have a sufficient foundation.

Word Recognition Development

Most students, especially those in kindergarten and first grade, benefit from systematic, explicit instruction in phonemic awareness and phonics knowledge (Adams 1990; NRP 2000; Snow, Burns, and Griffin 1998). Teaching students to hear the sounds in words and to blend these sounds into words are the two aspects of phonemic awareness that are most important for learning to read.

A variety of approaches to systematic phonics instruction are effective (Christensen and Bowey 2005; Juel and Minden-Cupp 2000: Mathes et al. 2005; NRP 2000), including letter-by-letter decoding and decoding by onset and rime. Coaching students to use word-recognition strategies as they read stories and informational texts is another important aspect of decoding instruction. For example, when Linda Garcia is listening to one student read and the student is stuck on a word, Linda says, "Start here, get your mouth ready." She asks, "What does this letter say?" The student gives the sound for the first letter. Linda asks about the sound for the second letter and then the third. The student comes up with the word. Linda reinforces the good work the student has done: "Wow! You stuck with it and came up with the word. Now go back and reread the sentence again so you're sure you understand the text."

Fluency Development

Developing *fluency*, or reading at a good rate with appropriate phrasing, is important since fluent reading supports comprehension. Oral reading procedures to develop fluency, in which students receive guidance or support, have a significant impact on students' reading abilities (Kuhn and Stahl 2003). Procedures to build fluency include repeated reading and coached reading, as well as ample opportunities to read just-right books. Effective reading instruction weaves fluency practice into whole-group and small-group lessons, as well as through independent work activities.

Vocabulary Development

When it comes to developing students' vocabulary, using a variety of approaches is critical. The approaches (Baumann and Kame'enui 2004; Blachowicz and Fisher 2000; Graves 2007) include:

▶ direct instruction in specific words

▶ prereading instruction in words

▶ learning to use strategies to determine word meanings

▶ learning of words in rich contexts and incidentally through wide reading

▶ studying words that children will find useful in many contexts (Beck, McKeown, and Kucan 2002)

Three points are worth emphasizing: First, some words need to be introduced before reading so that students are not confused about a major aspect of a story. When Heather Peterson and her students are reading a fable, "The Moon and the Well," she talks with students about the word *well* before they read. "Some of you might not know what a well is. Can anyone tell us?" Students are not sure so she explains, "A well is where you dig down into the earth to get fresh water."

Second, teachers sometimes do insufficient vocabulary instruction *during* the reading of a story. Beck and colleagues (2002) stress the value of teaching many word meanings at point of contact in the text. When Heather and her students are reading a *Weekly Reader* article about animal teeth, she talks about the meanings of unfamiliar words, such as *canine* teeth, as they come to them in the article.

Third, developing students' curiosity about words is also important. You can model this interest in word meanings and enthusiasm for authors' word choice in a variety of ways, and it's a boon to students' reading and writing. For example, Linda often has students use sticky notes to write down what she calls "juicy words" they come across as they read. She asks students to write down how these words are used in the story and what they mean. Later in the day, she asks students to share their "juicy words" at a whole-group meeting or in guided reading groups.

Comprehension Development

Skilled readers use strategies as they read to enhance their comprehension. Also, researchers have shown that instruction in comprehension strategies improves students' reading comprehension abilities (Pressley 2006; Guthrie, Wigfield, and VonSecker 2000; NRP 2000). Explicit lessons in the following strategies are most effective: summarizing; comprehension monitoring; use of graphic and semantic organizers before, during, and after reading; use of story structure; and question answering and question generation. Also, using multiple instructional strategies, like reciprocal teaching, in naturalistic contexts is important (Guthrie et al. 2004; Klingner et al. 2004; NRP 2000; Pressley

2006). The classroom examples that follow in Chapter 2 of Heather, John, and Linda exemplify instruction in comprehension strategies, including summarizing a story, summarizing information text, asking and answering questions, clarifying, and using multiple comprehension strategies.

Teaching students how to engage in high-level talk and writing about text is another vital aspect of comprehension instruction repeatedly found to be related to reading gains (Knapp 1995; McKeown, Beck, and Blake 2009; Saunders and Goldenberg 1999; Taylor et al. 2003; Van den Branden 2000). For example, after reading the fable, "The Crow and the Pitcher," Heather teaches students about the author's message when they discuss the meaning of the moral, "Little by little does the trick." Reflecting on the author's message or big ideas in a text allows readers to understand the story at a deeper level than simply recalling story events. First graders are often much more capable of high-level talk than teachers realize, and can make remarkable connections among texts, inferences, and statements about a story's big ideas and character motivation.

With these content elements under our belt, let's turn to the *how* behind the *what*: the essential pedagogy behind EIR lessons and all effective teaching.

Pedagogy: The Art of Teaching Demystified

You know good teaching when you see it, and yet it can be hard to capture all the nuances of it in the confines of a book. In short, it's all the routines and practices a teacher uses, as well as an ability to respond in the moment to students' needs and to connect to students so they feel motivated to learn. Some of these techniques include clearly stating lesson purposes or offering impromptu coaching, as well as making decisions about things such as timing (e.g., how long to spend on a particular aspect of a lesson) or what texts and tasks to use to engage students in purposeful learning activities.

Affective Dimension of Pedagogy: What It Means to Be Motivating to Kids

Another important aspect of pedagogy includes the people skills involved in teaching. Research and our own experiences have a lot to tell us about the impact of teachers' management, expectations, and attitudes toward learning on children's achievement and motivation. As you read the following list of effective classroom management characteristics and interaction practices, think about your first-grade students and how you view yourself on these aspects of effective teaching.

Having a good grasp of the content and pedagogy of effective reading instruction will inform your practice and support you in the many decisions you need to make in your day-to-day reading lessons. In turn, effective practices will help your students develop into motivated, competent readers.

Elements of Effective Pedagogy

Effective teachers skillfully coordinate many pedagogical aspects of their reading lessons. They make sure that they:

- Strike a good balance between whole-group and small-group instruction, using one form of grouping or another that best meets lesson objectives (Chorzempa and Graham 2006).

- Consider the purposes and timing of their lessons relative to their students' varying instructional needs.

- Balance direct teaching (telling, leading) with differentiated support (e.g., coaching, providing feedback) as students are engaged in learning activities (Connor, Morrison, and Katch 2004; Pressley et al. 2003; Taylor et al. 2003).

- Foster students' active involvement in literacy activities to enhance their learning and motivation (Guthrie et al. 2000).

- Use challenging, motivating activities for students when they are working with the teacher, on their own, or with other students (Pressley et al. 2003).

- Sustain a balanced approach to instruction that involves direct teaching of reading skills and strategies as well as giving students opportunities to apply skills and strategies to engaging texts through reading, writing, and discussing (Pressley 2006).

- Provide differentiated instruction and make good choices in the use of instructional materials based on students' abilities and interests (Pressley et al. 2007).

- Offer culturally responsive instruction, which includes teachers building on students' cultural strengths as they structure student interactions and as they use multicultural literature to celebrate students' cultural heritages and introduce students to new cultural perspectives (Au 2006).

- Assess students' engagement, understanding, and behavior throughout the day (Pressley et al. 2003).

- Systematically collect and share a variety of formal and informal student assessment data to help them make instructional decisions to improve student performance (Lipson et al. 2004; Taylor et al. 2000). Data might include diagnostic, formative (on-the-go assessment as kids work), and summative assessments (checking to see if students understand something at the end of learning).

Additional Motivating Pedagogical Practices

▶ Maintain positive classroom atmospheres and teach with enthusiasm for learning (Dolezal et al. 2003; Pressley et al. 2003).

▶ Expertly manage and organize their classrooms (Dolezal et al. 2003; Pressley 2001; Taylor, Pressley, and Pearson 2002).

▶ Provide encouragement and praise as well as positive feedback (Pressley 2006).

▶ Have high expectations for their students, communicate to students that effort leads to success, encourage independence and responsibility, provide for student choice and foster cooperative learning experiences (Bohn, Roehrig, and Pressley 2004; Dolezal et al. 2003; Guthrie et al. 2004; Hamre and Pianta 2005; Pressley et al. 2003).

▶ Collaborate with colleagues. While individual teachers can positively improve their reading instruction and thus the development of their students' reading, it is often helpful to work with colleagues as you embark on the journey of being the most effective teacher you can be. Heather, John, and Linda all believe that this collaboration piece is extremely instrumental to their success. John said, "The EIR study group was very helpful because teachers gave each other ongoing support. My colleagues have so many good ideas about structuring the reading block as well as ideas for challenging activities for independent work. We are a stronger team for being able to share our ideas." Linda said, "My teammates and I have started looking at what students are doing in a different way. We focus less on keeping them busy and more on how we can challenge and engage them with interesting and thought-provoking materials that get them to think and want to share with others."

A Three-Day Cycle of Supplemental Instruction

Now that we have looked at effective reading instruction for all students, lets turn to the EIR model for students who need extra support. The EIR model, like most other successful early intervention models (e.g., Reading Recovery [Clay 1993; Pinnell, Fried, and Eustice 1990]; Right Start [Hiebert et al. 1992]) is built on a strong research foundation. (See Pikulski 1994; Hiebert and Taylor 2000, for reviews of successful early reading intervention models.) It is important that emerging readers who are starting from a little behind quickly experience success in reading, and EIR is structured so this happens. The EIR model works on a three-day cycle. This predictable structure provides consistency for struggling readers, and helps build their confidence. During the three-day cycle of lessons, students are supported through the following practices:

- Active engagement

- Systematic word-recognition instruction

- Coaching in word-recognition strategies

- Repeated reading for fluency

- One-on-one reading practice

- Comprehension and vocabulary instruction

- Regular monitoring of progress

Active Engagement

Students are busy participating in reading experiences throughout the 20-minute, small-group session. Within this time period students engage in four activities that address different elements essential to learning to read. This 20-minute session is considered to be acceleration, unlike remediation, and implies that the children receiving this intervention can learn to read before they fall way behind. In other words, the intervention instruction accelerates their learning to read. In EIR, children typically enjoy the small-group routine and stay actively engaged during the lesson.

Systematic Word-Recognition Instruction

The teacher initially focuses on phonemic awareness development and an emphasis on letter-by-letter sequential decoding and progresses to an emphasis on decoding by onset and rime. Some phonemic awareness and phonics instruction is done through word work after students have read their EIR story, but another big emphasis is on coaching children to use multiple decoding strategies as they attempt to depend on themselves as they read the actual text. In a national study of accomplished teachers and effective schools, Taylor and colleagues (2000) found that phonics instruction in isolation is important but not sufficient. The best first- and second-grade teachers and teachers in the most effective schools were frequently observed coaching children in the use of word-recognition strategies as they got stuck on words while reading.

Coaching in Word-Recognition Strategies

While children read, teachers provide support through teacher modeling, asking questions, or giving prompts related to words children don't know how to decode. This coaching enables children to succeed at figuring out a word they don't instantly recognize while they are reading. Typically, when you ask children, "What do you do when you come to a word you don't know?" they will answer, "Sound it out." That is one good strategy, but we want them to realize there are other things readers do when they come to words they don't recognize. As coaches, we need to prompt children to use a variety of different word-recognition strategies and not overemphasize one single strategy so they learn they have a repertoire of strategies to use to decode words.

Coaching also helps children learn to self-monitor their word-recognition attempts. For example, if a child reads a word incorrectly, but then corrects it himself, this is a good example of self-monitoring. Complimenting children for their attempts (e.g., "Good checking, how did you know to try that word again?") is an integral part of the instruction, as the praise and questions keep

SOME RESEARCH-BASED LITERACY ACTIVITIES THAT ARE PART OF THE LESSONS

Elkonin Sound Boxes

This activity is used to develop phonemic awareness as well as letter-name knowledge, letter-sound knowledge, and letter-by-letter sequential decoding. Children listen for sounds in words from the stories they are reading and write the letters for these sounds in a string of boxes. For example, if a story is about a hen, the teacher asks students to listen for the sounds in the word *hen,* and, as they say the word, they write *h* in the first box, *e* in the second, and *n* in the third. This technique, along with the other word work activities discussed here, takes place after reading the story. (All of these techniques are described in more detail in Chapter 3.)

Cunningham's Making Words Technique

After about three months, teachers shift from Sound Boxes to Making Words (Cunningham 2009). In this activity, the teacher hands out letters to the students and asks them to build a word. The teacher asks them to place letters in front of them to make the first word she calls out, and they then change one or more letters at a time as they build different words and end up with a word from the story. In a story about thunder, students might create the words *net, ten, hen, den, nut, hut, thud,* and finally, *thunder*. Children learn to pay attention to the sequence of letters within words and the manipulating of the letter cards to spell the words the teacher calls out helps them grasp the alphabetic principle. At the end of the word-building activity, the teacher places cards for the words the children have made on the table and the children sort these words by first letter, and more important, by phonograms.

Guided Writing for Sounds

After reading, children write a sentence about the story as a group or with coaching support from the teacher. This writing is another important technique for providing word recognition instruction. After reading *The Carrot Seed* by Ruth Krauss (1945), students might write, "One day the seed came up." Students might need help from the teacher on writing down the *o* and *e* in *one*, the *y* in *day*, the second *e* in *seed*. By trying to write for sounds, as they also communicate an idea about the story, children refine their phonemic awareness, develop their understanding of the alphabetic principle, and learn letter-sound correspondences.

encouraging children to be aware of the strategies they are using to make sense of the text. Students will begin to notice instances when words they say don't make sense in the context of the story or don't look like the actual word they are trying to read. Part of self-monitoring is learning to cross-check; that is, not only being sure a word looks like the word on the page but also being sure that a word makes sense in the story, or vice versa.

Coaching in Word Recognition to Develop Student Independence

An important goal of coaching students in word-recognition strategies is to release responsibility to the children as soon as possible. Typically at first, you will have to model, or demonstrate for them, how to use different strategies. Also, you may have to suggest a particular strategy they might try for a particular word (e.g., "Is there a chunk you recognize?" Or, "Look at the picture." Or, "What would make sense?") or perhaps even start to use a strategy for them (e.g., sounding out the individual sounds, /p/ /a/, in *pat*.) Often, however, teachers inadvertently help struggling readers too much for too long, and the students don't learn to depend on themselves as readers. As the year progresses, you need to use more general prompts (e.g., "What can you do?" Or, "Look at that again.") and focus on your wait time to be sure you give students enough opportunity to try to problem solve and figure out words for themselves. When I am coaching children, I feel successful when they come to a hard word and don't look up at me for the answer. It's important to praise them for their independence and to remind them that this is what they need to continue to do when they are reading on their own.

Repeated Reading for Fluency

Students read and reread texts—a single book over three days. Over the three days they may read stories chorally, by taking turns in the small group, by reading with a partner, and by reading independently. This repeated reading helps them experience fluent reading as well as the feeling of success. Children also begin to develop automaticity for some of the high-frequency words they encounter in these stories (e.g., *the, is, and*).

The Benchmarks to Reach by Midyear and End of Year

You will read more about the transition phase of EIR in Chapter 5, but here is a brief preview: By February or March in first grade, the EIR routine alternates between repeated reading of a new story to transition reading for independence. (In some classes, the students in EIR will be ready to make the transition as early as mid-January; teachers need to use their professional judgment regarding this.) During transition reading, teachers work with two children at a time as they read a story for the first time. Teachers need to focus on being patient, giving enough wait time, and using general prompts as students attempt to use strategies when reading an unfamiliar text. It is important for the children to realize that they can pick up a book they have never read and actually read it and feel successful doing so. We want first-grade students to leave at the end of the school year with the feeling that they can continue to pick up books over the summer and read them successfully.

One-on-One Reading Practice

Another part of EIR that is essential for children's success is one-on-one coaching. As each child rereads their newest EIR story aloud, a coach is at his side listening, encouraging, and coaching. A coach can be an educational assistant, volunteer, or older student who has received training. With this individualized attention, the child is unable to hide behind someone else's voice and builds confidence in his or her ability to read. The student begins to build reading fluency and experiences success as a reader because she is reading some texts fluently.

Training one-on-one coaches is essential. See Chapter 8 for tips on training educational assistants, parents, community volunteers, and older students.

Comprehension and Vocabulary Instruction

Teaching beginning struggling readers to read for meaning is very important, but it is sometimes neglected because of the focus on teaching students to "break the code," or understand how to sound out words. To send the message that reading for meaning is what reading is all about, teachers in EIR lessons discuss the meanings of potentially unfamiliar words they come across in the story and ask one question about the story every day that either expands students' comprehension of the story, stretches their thinking, relates the story to their lives, or involves them in summarizing. As students answer questions that get them to think about the text, the teacher coaches them to elaborate on their ideas. I call this part of the EIR lesson "coaching for comprehension." Since there is a lot to cover in the 20-minute EIR lesson, teachers don't try to give all children a chance to answer a question every day. However, during the course of the three-day focus on a story, teachers are able to give all children a chance to answer one of the questions they ask.

Regular Monitoring of Progress

Finally, regular assessment of students' progress is important to their success in the EIR program and is a hallmark of effective teachers and schools (Lipson et al., 2004; Pressley et al. 2003; Taylor et al. 2000). Teachers need to monitor students' reading abilities frequently to know when to fine-tune their instruction. They may need to provide more help or they may need to release more responsibility to the students to accelerate their reading growth. The teacher takes an oral reading check about every other story on every student. (See Chapter 6 for more on assessment.) Based on research, first graders in EIR who are able to read a story with at least 90 percent accuracy after spending three days on it are making good progress in learning to read (Taylor et al. 1992).

Oral reading checks are difficult to analyze for patterns of errors in first grade when the children are in the repeated reading phase of the EIR model because students often have parts of the story memorized. A teacher may get an inaccurate picture of the errors students would make if they were reading more independently. By the transition phase, however, teachers can begin to analyze oral reading errors. (This is described in more detail in Chapter 5.)

How the EIR Model Fits Within a Balanced Literacy Block

Now, let's take a look at how you might fit EIR lessons into your day by organizing your instruction around a 110- to 120-minute reading block.

Reading Block: A Sample Schedule

Heather Peterson has a 120-minute reading block. She spends about 25 minutes a day on a whole-group lesson with a 5-minute sharing on follow-up activities related to this lesson at the end of the literacy block. She spends about 60 minutes a day on three guided reading groups and 20 minutes on one EIR group (the second shot of quality instruction for her struggling readers). See the next page for an example of her schedule.

In the next chapter, you'll see how Heather and two other teachers make the content and pedagogy of effective reading instruction—and the principles of EIR—come alive in their whole-group and small-group lessons. In Chapters 3 and 5, we look at excellent reading instruction again so you can see it through the lens of the intervention lessons. We also look at effective techniques for managing the reading block, including EIR lessons and independent work activities, in Chapter 7.

Reading Block: Heather's Sample Schedule

9:00–9:25 Whole-Group Lesson

- ◗ Use a selection from basal reader or a trade book
- ◗ Target a comprehension strategy
- ◗ Teach vocabulary at point of contact in the selection
- ◗ Pose and discuss answers to high-level questions
- ◗ Review learning activities for independent work time

9:25–10:45 Independent and Small-Group Work

Independent Work: While the teacher is working with small groups of students, the other students are working independently or with a partner or small group on challenging and differentiated materials. (See Chapter 7 for a more in-depth discussion of independent work activities.) For example, students might:

- ◗ Read new texts as directed by the teacher
- ◗ Write in a journal or on open-ended response sheets about what they have read
- ◗ Talk with others about what they have read
- ◗ Write down new or interesting vocabulary and possible word meanings
- ◗ Read/reread books in their book baskets or book bags

Small-Group 1 (9:25–9:45)

Using a story in a text at students' reading level, the teacher will

- ◗ Provide phonics instruction as needed
- ◗ Coach students in word-recognition strategies as they read their leveled text
- ◗ Discuss vocabulary at point of contact in the story
- ◗ Provide follow-up instruction to the comprehension strategy targeted in whole-group lesson
- ◗ Pose and discuss answers to high-level questions on leveled text

Small-Group 2 (9:45–10:05)

Follow the same strategies as small group 1.

Small-Group 3 (10:05–10:25)

Follow the same strategies as small group 1.

EIR lesson (10:25–10:45)

Follow EIR strategies. (Note that these students were also in small groups 1, 2, or 3.)

10:50–11:00 Whole-Class Follow-up to Whole-Class Lesson

Based on activities completed during independent work time, Heather and her students discuss answers to questions, interesting vocabulary, and comprehension strategies practiced from the text they worked on during their whole-group lesson.

Meet the Teachers

The Differentiated Lessons and
Teacher Collaboration That
Support EIR

Heather Peterson, John Luther, and Linda Garcia—the teachers highlighted in this chapter—are connected to my Early Intervention in
Reading (EIR) framework and to my work on effective instruction
and school change in reading (Taylor 2010c). All three teachers taught EIR
lessons to their students who needed more reading support, regularly
demonstrated elements of effective instruction during their reading lessons,
and participated in school-based reading improvement efforts. Before we
turn to the details of teaching EIR lessons I share vignettes from their reading

Diversity in the Highlighted Teachers' Schools

Teacher	Years Teaching	School Setting	Percent of Students Who Receive Subsidized Lunch	Percent of English Language Learners
Heather	15	Suburban	36	9
John	3	Urban	65	28
Linda	22	Inner city	86	56

Table 2-1 Diversity in the Highlighted Teachers' Schools

lessons to paint a backdrop for the EIR lessons, so you see how one supports and echoes the reading content and pedagogy of the other. I also share quotes from these teachers about the benefits of engaging in professional development with colleagues. You can help your struggling readers more if you can take on EIR as a group, whether it's teachers at your grade level, in the primary grades, or schoolwide. These three teachers teach in different schools with different student populations and needs. Table 2-1 above highlights this diversity.

The Teachers

Heather Peterson teaches first grade at Northridge Elementary, a suburban school where 36 percent of the students receive subsidized lunch and 9 percent speak English as a second language. Heather has been teaching for fifteen years, participated in study groups as part of a schoolwide reading improvement project for three years, and learned how to deliver EIR instruction for students in need of more reading support in one of these study groups. During this time, the students in Heather's class improved each year, on average, from the 56th to the 68th percentile on the Gates MacGinitie standardized reading test.

John Luther teaches first grade at Roosevelt Elementary, an urban school where 65 percent of the students receive subsidized lunch and 28 percent are ESL students, primarily native Spanish speakers. John has been teaching for three years, and he learned how to teach EIR lessons during his third year. The students in his class went from the 34th to 45th percentile, on average, on the Gates MacGinitie standardized reading test between fall and spring.

Linda Garcia teaches first grade at Wheeler Elementary, an inner-city school where 86 percent of the students receive subsidized lunch and 56 percent are ESL students, including native Spanish, Somali, and Hmong speakers. Linda has been teaching for twenty-two years, and she learned how to teach EIR lessons in the second year of her school's reading reform project. During that year, her class' reading scores improved from the 27th to the 40th percentile, on average, on the Gates MacGinitie standardized reading test.

Common Factors in Heather, John, and Linda's Reading Instruction

While each of these teachers has a different style and works in a different setting, there are similarities that are instrumental to the success of their teaching and the reading achievement of their students. Heather, for example, cites the following components as critical to the success of her classroom reading program:

▶ Teaching reading with a focus on meaning

▶ Providing sufficient modeling, coaching, and guided practice

▶ Giving students many opportunities to respond and participate

▶ Differentiating instruction

▶ Using the EIR model with students who come to her in the fall at risk of falling behind in reading in first grade

▶ Providing students with independent work that is appropriate for their level as readers, is engaging, and is designed to deepen their understanding. That is, not easy busywork!

▶ Collaborating with other teachers in teaching and in professional learning

Similarly, John believes that his reading instruction became more powerful after he made an effort to focus on comprehension and higher-level thinking. The small-group work, he says, is instrumental in targeting learners' individual needs.

Linda attributes her success to many of these components too, and emphasizes that another key reason for her students' success is that she began to use far more informational texts in her teaching than before. She weaves nonfiction throughout the reading block, using it instructionally and as part of students' independent reading.

Teacher Talk

The quotes that follow are meant to cheerlead you as you embark on learning to teach EIR lessons as one aspect of your classroom reading program. Whether you are a beginning or veteran teacher, the implementation of EIR will help your struggling readers make good growth in reading during their first-grade year. Read what these teachers had to say when I asked them how professional learning, including EIR, changed their instruction.

The Influence of Collaborative Professional Learning on Teaching Practice

HEATHER: My teaching is more differentiated and based on student needs. I use more modeling and coaching for all students. I focus more on comprehension and my students do more active responding to text. I have a lot more confidence in the students and therefore higher expectations. I have a lot more confidence in myself as a teacher by going through our school reading improvement process.

JOHN: I teach a lot more strategies and I'm more aware about higher-level questions and differentiating my instruction. I think sticking with comprehension instruction and teaching students to think about their own thinking when it comes to strategies for comprehension has been a real shift in the way I teach. Another change is more small-group work, which I added based on EIR strategies.

LINDA: I use much more informational text and teach word recognition and comprehension strategies that I never taught before. I also realize that vocabulary is so important and I had not emphasized it enough. The biggest way I have changed is to allow and encourage students to become more independent. I have much higher expectations and students rise to them. My pacing has improved as well. I am moving guided reading groups to the reading table and back to their seats faster than I used to, and I also move students to different groups more often.

Notice that these teachers mentioned differentiation, small-group work, having high expectations of students, and allowing students to be active and independent learners as important changes they had made to their reading instruction in recent years. These are all essential elements of effective pedagogy

Biggest Benefits to Student Learning

When asked about the biggest benefits to student learning, the teachers had similar responses.

HEATHER: My instruction is more individualized than in the past, and I think this makes a big difference in my students' achievement. I've seen lots of growth in my struggling readers' fluency, and I think the EIR process has contributed to this growth. Also, all my students do more active responding to text.

JOHN: I'm not seeing my low kids floundering as much. They've got a sense that they can be successful in reading. I had not seen this before I started to implement EIR. All of my students are on task 99 percent of the time. They are working, engaged, and participating in class, so I have fewer behavior problems.

LINDA: I see my students as being independent readers who are confident and making good progress. I see that my students like reading, they choose to read, and they talk about their reading with others. I think this is a result of fine-tuning my instruction and looking at what my students' needs are and trying to meet those needs.

Biggest Challenges

When asked about the biggest challenges to teach their first graders, the teachers' honest responses are probably not so surprising to you. The challenges include issues of classroom management; dips in confidence about their ability to meet each child's needs, especially those of their struggling readers and English language learners (ELLs); and ensuring activities are interesting and challenging.

HEATHER: I think for me, the most challenging things are planning for and getting to all of my small groups and making sure students' independent work is differentiated and challenging.

JOHN: I think one of the most difficult things is that so many children are coming in not at grade level. A lot of them come from non-English speaking homes, so they don't have the English language skills of traditional first graders.

LINDA: Ensuring that students are all actively engaged and learning and providing students with independent work is challenging. My teammates and I have started looking at what students are doing in a different way. We focus less on keeping them busy and more on what they are doing that is interesting and getting them to think and share with others.

On the following pages detailed descriptions of Heather's, John's, and Linda's reading instruction provide examples of what effective reading instruction looks like in practice. Notice how the teachers integrate the various components of content including instruction in word recognition, fluency, vocabulary, and comprehension, as well as elements of pedagogy including direct teaching and coaching; differentiation; and intellectually challenging independent, partner, and small-group activities.

I want to emphasize that the beauty of EIR is that it can reside in many different kinds of classrooms, complementing a reading workshop approach or any other balanced literacy model. As you read these lesson overviews, remember they don't capture every teaching move but are here to show you how different teachers incorporate elements of effective reading instruction, including EIR lessons, into their teaching based on their own styles and, of course, their students' needs.

Sample Lesson
Summarizing a Story and Identifying the Author's Message

Heather Peterson's reading block was described at the end of Chapter 1. Below are highlights from one of her lessons.

Summarizing a Story and Identifying the Author's Message

Whole-Group Lesson

In February, Heather works on the comprehension strategy of summarizing a story, and including the author's message in that summary. She and her first graders read a fable, *The Crow and the Pitcher*. She says, "We summarize a story by talking about the character and setting in the beginning, the problem in the middle, and the solution in the end. We also want to include the author's message at the end of our summary." Heather reads the fable as students follow along. Then, the children write their ideas on their story maps as the teacher writes on the whiteboard about the beginning, middle, end of the story, and author's message.

Partner Work Within a Whole-Group Lesson

Heather has students talk with a partner about the meaning of the moral of the story. She also asks them to make a text-to-self connection by talking with a partner about a time they had a problem, just like the crow had a problem in the story, and tell how the problem was solved. Some pairs then share their ideas with the class.

Independent Follow-Up Work

Heather makes a transition to independent work time. She continues, "Now flip your paper over. There is another story map on the back. I am going to give you a story of your own to work on with a partner during independent work time. Read it carefully and think about what the author wants you to know. Include the character and setting in the beginning, the story problem in the middle, and the solution and author's message at the end." The teacher differentiates by giving students books based on their reading level, *Legend of Blue Bonnet* for the above-average readers, *The Man and the Donkey* for the average readers, and *Five Silly Fisherman* for the below-average readers.

Later, during independent work time, students read these stories with a partner and complete their own story maps. Students share their work with their partner and turn it in to the teacher so she can assess students' progress in writing a summary on a story map. If students complete this activity, they have other activities to accomplish. For example, students might read informational texts and respond in their response journals by

 **tips**

Partner Work

While some teachers choose partners randomly, others are more deliberate. The teachers who are more deliberate try to partner students who will be able to support each other while they work. Switching the partners every two or three weeks also works well. This way, students get more experience working with different types of learners.

writing about the new information they learned. Also, students might read from their independent reading books.

Small-Group Lesson

On the same day that Heather works with her students in a whole-group lesson on summarizing a story and understanding the author's message, she continues to work on the author's message in a small group of advanced readers. The students have the book, *Fables from Around the World*. She explains, "Since we are talking about the author's big ideas this week, we are going to read more stories called *fables* from the book, *Fables from Around the World*. Fables have a message—or moral—the author wants you to know. We will be reading *The Moon and the Well*."

At the end of reading the tale, students summarize the beginning, middle, and end of the fable and discuss the moral with coaching from their teacher. Heather asks, "What is the big idea?" A student answers, "It is teamwork." Heather asks, "Did it work in this story?" Students shake their heads. Students seem stuck, so Heather says, "I will model what I am thinking is the author's purpose. The leader was trying to get them to get together and work as a team, but he tried to make them do something that was not good. Is it okay to stand up to a leader if they are leading you in a wrong direction?" Students say, "Yeah." After more discussion, they come up with the following for the moral, or author's message, "Don't follow the leader if it's a bad decision." The teacher tells students they will go back and read another story in the book and then do their big idea map.

Small-Group Intervention Lesson

When Heather works with her EIR students, she also helps them work on summarizing their EIR story, *Herman the Helper* (Kraus 1974). She tells them, "We are going to think about the beginning, middle, and end of this story when we summarize and also the author's message just like we did today in whole group." Heather gives students a folded paper book she made that students will use to summarize their story (see Appendix 4-1), and she reads the first page, which has a sentence summarizing the beginning of *Herman the Helper* already written on it. Heather asks student to draw a picture to match the words she reads. On the next page, students are to write a sentence about someone who Herman liked to help from the middle of the story. On the third page of the book, students are to write a sentence about the end of the story and the author's message. Heather asks, "How did this end?" A student answers, "He ate dinner." Heather coaches the student to elaborate. "Did he need anyone to help him or could he do it all by himself? Do you feel good when you do something all by yourself? How do you think Herman felt?" Students write, "Herman helped himself and he felt good." Heather asks students to read their summaries.

Whole-Group Share

At the end of the reading block, Heather calls the class together and a few students share their summaries and discuss how summarizing and thinking about the author's message enabled them to better understand and appreciate the text.

If you want to read more lessons to help you get ideas about the complex task of integrating the many aspects of effective reading instruction into your teaching, you will find there are two more lessons by Heather in Appendices 2-1 and 2-2 available in the DVD teacher resources. One focuses on the comprehension strategy of asking and answering questions and one focuses on the comprehension strategy of summarizing informational text. Looking across these three lessons, Heather provides excellent, differentiated instruction as she teaches a comprehension strategy with a whole group and reinforces this strategy in guided reading groups. Her instruction is intellectually challenging, students' independent activities are motivating and require high-level thinking, and students are actively engaged. These lessons also offer good examples of collaborative work and student choice.

John Luther has a 110-minute reading block. He begins with a whole-group lesson that lasts about 20 minutes. He then spends about 45 minutes on three guided reading groups and 20 minutes on one EIR group, which is a second shot of quality instruction for his struggling readers. He has an educational assistant in his classroom during his reading block who listens to EIR students reread their stories and provides assistance during students' independent work time.

Teaching a Sound for the Letter *I*

In the fall, John does some decoding instruction with the whole group and follows up on this in small, guided reading groups. Later in the year, when some advanced readers no longer need much in the way of explicit phonics instruction but other students do, he provides most of his decoding instruction in small groups to best meet students' varying needs.

In a November lesson, John reads a story about animals getting ready for winter. He reviews the purpose of learning phonics with his whole group. He asks, "Why is it so important to know our letter sounds?" Students say, "To help us read." John coaches his students to elaborate, "Why do letter sounds help us read?" One student tries to explain, "We use the sounds in letters." John elaborates, "We use letter sounds to help us sound out words, and we sound out words all our lives. I still do that today when I come to a hard word I haven't seen before. Today, we are going to focus on words with the short *i*, the sound you hear in *igloo*." He points to the picture of an igloo on a short vowel chart. "The letter *i* can say /i/ as in *igloo*. You say it with me, /i/ as in *igloo*. If you come to this word (*it*), you sound it out as /i/ /t/ /it/. If you come to this word (*sit*), you sound it out as /s/ /i/ /t/ /sit/. In our story today, we read about fish and crickets." He writes these words on the board. "Let's sound out this word, /f/ /i/ /sh/. Sometimes *i* can say /long i/ and sometimes it can say /short i/. In this word, it is /i/." He sounds out *cricket* for them. "In our small groups today, we will write words with short *i* in them." John reads the story aloud to the class, stopping to check for understanding, pointing out short *i* words, and also to explain the meanings of words with which students might not be familiar.

Small Groups

John differentiates his phonics instruction on short *i* in his three guided reading groups. With the average group, he has them write short *i* words in sound boxes, *fish*, *dish*, *lick*, and *sick*. He has the students say the words themselves and write the sounds in boxes. He points out that *sh* and *ck* go in one box because they make one sound. He also talks about the word families of *ish* and *ick* and how recognizing a word family can help you sound out the word.

With his lowest-ability group, he also has them write words with short *i* in sound boxes, but he uses simpler words like, *fit, sit, dig,* or *fish*. He sounds out the words for the students as they write the letters for the sound in sound boxes. He does not talk about word families with short *i* at this time, but will do so in a lesson later in the week. He also focuses on short *i* with those students who are in his EIR group.

With his highest-ability group, John has students write harder words like *river, cricket,* and *spider* that come from the story about animals getting ready for winter. He talks about decoding multisyllabic words. "When you sound out words, you need to be flexible with the sounds you try. The letter *i* can say /short i/ or it can say /long i/. When you sound out a word with *i* in it, if one sound doesn't work, try the other sound. In *spider* it is the long *i* sound. In *river* it is the short *i* sound."

In Appendix 2-3 on the DVD resources, there is one more lesson by John that focuses on using multiple comprehension strategies. John provides excellent examples of differentiated instruction in his phonics lesson and does a good job of clearly stating lesson purposes in both examples.

Sample Lesson
Differentiating Her Approach to Summarizing Narratives

Linda Garcia has a 120-minute reading block each day. She spends about 30 minutes a day on a whole-group lesson in the morning and about 65 minutes with three guided reading groups. After lunch, she spends 20 minutes on one EIR group as the other students complete independent work or engage in reading for pleasure from books of their own choosing. Linda has an educational assistant in her room in the morning during small-group time and an ELL teacher as well who works with two small groups of students.

Differentiating Her Approach to Summarizing Narratives

Linda's class has been working on summarizing texts as a way to develop and deepen comprehension. In the following lessons, Linda works with several groups during reading center time. Each of the groups works on summarizing a story but with different books and different methods.

Beginning, Middle, and End

Linda first works with her students who are not yet reading on grade level. She hands out new books to the group at the reading table. Students start reading their books. Linda listens to one student read and takes a running record. The student struggles with a word. Linda praises him when he decodes the word correctly: "Good work! I like how you stuck with it and figured it out." Linda says to the group, "We are going to read the rest of the book together, and then we're going to do an activity. But first, I want us to read and practice our fluency." She reads through the last few pages with the students. She reminds different students to track as they read because this is still helpful for these struggling readers at this point in the year. However, she does not recommend tracking with her average and above-average readers because it is now a crutch they no longer need and it slows them down.

Linda shows the group a paper with events from the book written on it. She says, "We are going to read these sentences and then decide, what happened first, second, and then at the end." She hands out the papers and students cut out their strips. Linda reads through the strips with one student, asking him to put them in order. She then reads a strip with another student and asks, "Where does it go, beginning, middle, or end?" The student says it goes at the beginning. Linda listens to a few more students read through their strips that summarize the story and helps them sound out words that they don't know. When one student isn't sure where to put a strip, she coaches, "Look back in your book." She praises one student by saying, "Look, Marcus is looking back in his book to figure out where the sentence strips go." She continues to help students order their strips and reread them to summarize their story (active responding). Later in the month, she teaches these students to summarize in their own words in writing.

Expecting More Independence

Linda's next small group is made up of students who are average readers. She uses a different approach that challenges students to do more of the summarizing on their own. After students read their story by themselves, she hands out a story map and says, "Will you tell us what happened at the beginning, so that we can start making a summary? Remember to tell about the main characters, the setting, and the problem." A student tells what happened in his own words. Linda has the students write about the beginning on their story maps. She then asks, "Tell us what happened in the middle. What were the events related to the problem?" A student shares a summary in her own words. Then Linda says, "I want you to finish your story map at your seats. Write down in your own words what happened in the middle and at the end. Remember to put the solution to the problem and the big idea, or author's message, at the end. We'll take a look at what you wrote when we meet tomorrow."

In Appendix 2-4 on the DVD resources there is a second lesson by Linda that focuses on vocabulary at point of contact and after reading. Linda provides a good example of differentiated instruction in her lesson on summarizing a story. She regularly offers positive, enthusiastic feedback. Students are actively engaged by sharing with a partner, sometimes seen crossing their arms during the vocabulary lesson.

@ @ @

In Chapter 7, we return to Heather, John, and Linda's classrooms. We learn about their daily reading schedules that include the EIR lessons they provide to their students who need more support. We also learn about the motivating, independent learning activities they set up for their students to engage in as they work with guided reading and EIR groups.

Making a Schoolwide Commitment to
First-Grade Readers

Before we jump in to the EIR lessons how-tos, let's take a moment to think about your own school, and how you might collaborate with one or more of your colleagues on this venture.

The best teaching possible arises from schools in which teachers develop a shared set of understandings and beliefs about teaching and learning in general, and teaching reading in particular. Considerable research in the last decade has identified the following characteristics of schoolwide reading programs that support teachers' abilities to increase students' reading abilities. These schools have

- A unified vision for teaching reading in every grade and a cohesive, schoolwide program (Taylor, Raphael, and Au in press; Taylor et al. 2005)

- A substantial number of minutes and designated blocks of time devoted to reading instruction across different grades (Taylor et al. 2000)

- A schoolwide assessment plan in which student data is collected and used regularly to inform instruction (Pressley et al. 2003; Taylor et al. 2000; Taylor, Pressley, and Pearson 2002)

- Interventions in place to meet the needs of students who are experiencing reading difficulties, who have special education needs, and who are English language learners (Foorman and Torgesen 2001; Mathes et al. 2005; Taylor et al. 2000)

- Effective parent partnerships (Edwards 2004; Taylor, Pressley, and Pearson 2002)

It is ideal to have an effective schoolwide reading program in place, whereby a common vision, time to work together, and a culture of peer support are part of your school's culture, and yet, an individual teacher working hard on her own to enhance her practice can make a huge difference in the lives of the students in her class. Nevertheless, keep in mind that as Heather, John, Linda, and so many other teachers will attest, working with colleagues can provide amazing support. It's hard to examine and critique your own practice. Trusted colleagues can watch you teach, give you feedback, point out your strengths, and offer ideas to enhance your instruction in certain areas. This support helps you look closely at your practice, make modifications, and in the end, teach as effectively as possible so all of your students become skilled, motivated readers. In Chapter 8 I provide more details on how to set up monthly sessions with colleagues, teach educational assistants or volunteers how to serve as one-on-one coaches, and enlist the support of parents in their children's learning-to-read efforts. Consider exploring the content, pedagogy, and interpersonal skills of exemplary teachers further. Professional books and research articles abound on many of the components of effective reading instruction discussed in this chapter and in Chapter 1. See the Recommended Professional Readings in the reference section at the back of this book.

3

The Three-Day Lesson Routine

• •

Now, let's look at the daily routines of EIR lessons, the rationale behind them, and some basic information to get you started. I'm putting a lot of my advice in bulleted lists because I encourage you to dip in and out of this book as you launch EIR. First, let's review four foundational ideas:

▶ With EIR, you accelerate students' reading progress based on the same effective reading instruction you use with all students—this is not about remediation.

▶ Students who are struggling with reading get an extra shot of quality, small-group reading instruction. These children are getting this support in addition to—not instead of—other whole-group, small-group and one-on-one attention.

▶ Engaging children's books are chosen for the lessons (see the list of sample books in in Chapter 4 [Table 4-2] to guide you).

▶ Children who come to first grade with relatively weak letter–sound knowledge and phonemic awareness get the help they need. With solid intervention lessons, these children are likely to become independent readers in first grade.

Getting Started: FAQs

In Chapter 6, you will find more information on determining which children might benefit from EIR. But for now, here are some questions teachers commonly ask about setting up the groups.

How many students are in a group?

Each group should have about five to seven students, seven being the maximum. If there are more than seven children in your room who need EIR lessons, I would recommend finding a way to have two groups instead of just one. If you have Title 1 at your school, perhaps the Title 1 teacher can take one group and you can take the other. Then you can periodically switch groups so you have a sense of the strengths and weaknesses of all your readers who need additional support to become successful.

What if I have a bunch of first graders who need EIR?

With two EIR groups, teachers find it works well to put the faster-progressing students in one group and the slower-progressing students in the other. This grouping allows for all learners to learn at about the same pace; the faster-moving students won't call out answers at the expense of the slower-moving students. Also, the slower-moving students are less inclined to feel discouraged if they do not experience others in their group catching on more quickly.

The students in the faster-progressing group may include a student who will be taken out of EIR before the end of the school year because they have benefited from EIR lessons and are reading on grade level. Guidelines to help you decide if a child no longer needs EIR lessons are provided in Chapter 6.

Who should teach the EIR students?

As hard as it is to teach two EIR groups, should you find you need to do this, I cannot recommend that one of the groups be taught by an instructional aide. Children at risk of reading failure desperately need quality, supplemental reading instruction, which is in addition to instruction from the regular reading program, and which is provided by certified teachers.

What advice do you have in regard to English language learners and EIR?

Often the question comes up as how to handle English language learners (ELLs) and fall placement in EIR. It is true that ELLs, especially children such as Hmong students whose first language sounds are very different from English, will score more poorly on the phonemic awareness assessment than would be the case if they were native English speakers. On the other hand, even if ELLs do relatively poorly on the fall assessment, I would put them in an EIR group in the fall unless they have the opportunity to learn to read in their first language. If possible, I might use something like the kindergarten EIR program (Taylor forthcoming; also see Lessons for Students Who Need Additional Phonemic Awareness Instruction in Appendix 3-1) to develop oral vocabulary and emergent literacy skills at the same time, but not instead of, their participation in first-grade EIR lessons. You do not want to take the chance of preventing any student from learning to read by postponing their participation in EIR to a later time, such as after the first of the year. Also, I have found that ELL students generally do well in EIR (Taylor 2001).

How do special education students fare with EIR?

I have also found that EIR works well with students with learning disabilities. No modifications to the program are recommended.

However, students who are developmentally and cognitively delayed learn well in EIR, but more predictable texts are typically needed than those used in regular EIR lessons to keep the children feeling successful. I would start out with the regular books at EIR Level A and switch to more predictable books, if needed, because the regular EIR stories at Levels B and C get longer and harder. EIR book levels are discussed in Chapter 4 and described in Table 4-1.

Do the children in EIR groups feel stigmatized?

Over the many years I've been implementing and researching EIR, teachers report that this is not the case. In fact, children love the fast pace, interesting stories, and feelings of success that they experience in EIR lessons. Children who no longer need EIR lessons because they are reading on grade level often do not want to give the group up. All children are in small groups with their teacher, so no one seems to think much about who is with the teacher when. But the children in EIR lessons like the extra time with their teacher if she is the one teaching the EIR group.

What's the optimum time of the year to start EIR?

It is best to begin EIR in October. However, if you have just bought or been given this book and it is February, then for you, February would be the best time to begin. For a February start, you would begin with books at EIR Level C. If these books are too challenging because you have not had students in EIR in the fall, you may have to drop back to Level B books. However, one of the major problems I have seen in the hundreds of first-grade classrooms I have visited over the past 20 years is that teachers often have their students, and especially their struggling readers, reading books that are too easy for them. Remember, in the EIR model we want to challenge students and get them to "glue to the print" so they can figure out how to sound out words as quickly as possible so they can understand new vocabulary and gain meaning from text.

What's the best way for me to begin to build my confidence with EIR?

After you read through the three-day set of procedures for the basic first-grade teaching routines in Figure 3-1, read the detailed Day 1 procedures that follow and watch the corresponding Day 1 video clips on the accompanying DVD. Soon, the EIR routines will seem very natural, and, as many teachers have reported, you will feel that the extra work on your part is worth the effort! For the past twenty years, I have consistently found that teachers, by February, are very excited about the progress they see their struggling readers making.

How do I know when I am ready to actually teach the lessons?

Once you have read this book, you may not feel completely ready to conduct the lessons, but I have found the best way to learn about EIR procedures is to just jump in and try them. If you have questions, and I'm sure you will, you can reread parts of the book or rewatch particular video clips. Ideally, you will be working with a group of colleagues learning and implementing EIR together so that you can share successes and discuss questions and uncertainties together.

Grade 1 Basic EIR Procedures

DAY 1 LESSON

1. Group rereads a familiar, old story for fluency. Teacher conducts oral reading check or coaches in word recognition.

2. Teacher reads from "new" book and models a variety of word-recognition strategies for three to five words from the story. Teacher discusses meanings of some unfamiliar words with students at point of contact in the story. Children reread story chorally.

3. Teacher coaches for comprehension and discusses meaning of other unfamiliar words not discussed in Step 2.

4. Group completes Sound Box or Making Words activity.

DAY 2 LESSON

1. Group rereads familiar, old story again for fluency. Teacher conducts oral reading check or coaches in word recognition.

2. Group rereads "new" story twice while the teacher coaches as needed.

3. Teacher coaches for comprehension.

4. Group writes a sentence about the story and the teacher gives support as needed. Each child should be engaged in hearing the sounds in the words and in trying to write the letters for these sounds. The students should not be simply copying a sentence as the teacher writes it.

DAY 3 LESSON

1. Group rereads old story for fluency. Teacher conducts oral reading check or coaches in word recognition.

2. Group rereads "new" story twice while the teacher coaches as needed.

3. Teacher coaches for comprehension.

4. Group writes a second sentence about the story and the teacher gives support as needed. Each child should be engaged in hearing the sounds in the words and in trying to write the letters for these sounds. The students should not be simply copying a sentence as the teacher writes it.

Figure 3-1 Grade 1 Basic EIR Procedures*

* It's helpful to keep this form at your side during EIR lessons. Photocopy for easy reference.

Day 1
Lesson Routine

Every day you and your group of five to seven children will reread "old" EIR stories (that is, those stories read in previous EIR lessons), read the current story, work on comprehension, and do word work or sentence writing. You need to pay careful attention to your timing to get through these four activities in 20 minutes (or 30 minutes at first). I always tell teachers that if they take longer than 20 to 25 minutes, they may be tempted to quit doing EIR because it seems to take up too much time. So try to stay within the 20-minute time frame.

Overview of the Lesson Steps

1. Group members read stories they have read before in EIR lessons for fluency. Typically, the teacher gives them a number of the most recent books to read and they select the ones they like the best. The teacher conducts an oral reading check or coaches in word recognition.

2. Teacher reads from a new book and models a variety of word-recognition strategies for three to five words from the story. The teacher discusses meanings of some unfamiliar words with students at point of contact in the story. Children reread the story chorally.

3. Teacher coaches for comprehension and discusses meaning of other unfamiliar words not discussed in Step 2.

4. Teacher develops phonemic awareness and phonics with Sound Box or Making Words activity.

Day 1, Step 1: Reread Old Stories
(5 min.)

Take the first few minutes of the lesson to build children's confidence as they reread "old" stories by themselves or with a partner. (I call them *old* stories because it's easier for young children to understand than calling them *familiar* stories.) You will work with one student on word recognition during this phase. Rereading familiar stories gives the children time to experience fluent reading and success. Also, they are building a sight vocabulary as they reread familiar words. (See Chapter 4, Table 4-2, for a list of the kinds of authentic literature children will be reading.)

In the beginning, you'll need to remind your first graders to keep from telling their partner a word and to give them a hint instead. Since a major emphasis in EIR is on coaching children to be independent, you don't want a partner calling out a word when a child gets stuck. Guide students to use the following prompts with their reading partner.

Prompts Students Can Give During Partner Reading

It starts with . . . (child gives his reading partner the beginning sound).

This part says . . . (child provides his partner with a rhyming part like *at* or *op*).

Look at the picture . . .

Look at this word again . . . (for child who misreads a word).

What the Teacher Does

Use this rereading time to conduct an oral reading check (described in Chapter 6) with one child, coach a child who is having difficulty catching on to reading, or rotate among students in the group, listening to them read and coaching them in word recognition as needed. You can use the following prompts when coaching students to use word-recognition strategies.

Prompts Teachers Can Use to Coach Students to Use Word-Recognition Strategies

Self-Monitoring Prompts

Good checking! How did you know it wasn't . . . ?

You said . . . . Does that make sense? Does that look and sound right?

Why did you stop? What did you notice?

Decoding Prompts

What can you do to figure out that word?

What word starts with the letter ___ and would make sense?

Is there a rhyming part you recognize?

Can you sound it out and come up with a word that makes sense?

Let's start again from the beginning of the sentence to see if this word makes sense.

See it in Action

DAY 1
Reading an Old Story

On Day 1, first-grade teacher Celia Huxley begins by having students reread the story they just spent three days on, a summary of *Herman the Helper.* (In this example, because of budget constraints, the teacher had previously read the entire book to the students and then wrote a summary of the story on chart paper and on sheets she folded into little books. Ideally, children would have the actual published books.) Students read with a partner as she coaches one student. Celia says, "I want Nick and Shaun to be partners. Nick reads the first page and Shaun reads the second. Then, when you are done, you read it again, although this time Shaun goes first and then Nick. I also want Jake and Akouma to be partners. As you read, I'm going to listen to Andy read." Celia listens to Andy read the summary of *Herman the Helper*, but she also pays attention to the other students at the same time. She reminds Akouma to track the words with her finger as she reads and to listen to Jake as he is reading. When Andy gets stuck on the word *himself* but knows *him*, she coaches, "Cover up the first part." She puts her finger over *him*, and Andy quickly comes up with *himself*.

Day 1, Step 2: Read a New Story

(5 min.)

Read It Aloud

On Day 1, it is important for you, the teacher, to read aloud the new story to the children first so that you can track for them. That is, insist they follow the words you are reading with their eyes. Plan to pause on four to five words and to think aloud about a few strategies for figuring out unfamiliar words. Briefly discuss the meaning of unfamiliar words. Since you have a small group of students, you can read from your book as opposed to a big book, but you need to make sure students are positioned so they can follow along.

   In this segment of the lesson, some of the word-recognition strategies you might model are:

▶ Use the first letter sound plus thinking of what would make sense. (Note, you only use this at the beginning of the year. Later you want students to decode from the beginning to the end of a word.)

- Look for a chunk.

- Sound out each letter and blend the sounds together.

- Cross-check for meaning—make sure the word makes sense in the text.

- Reread after working on a word because this helps readers understand and remember what is read.

Choral Read

After you read aloud the story to the children, read it again with them chiming in.

see it iN ActioN

Decoding Strategies

After reading the old story, Celia reads the "new" story with her group. First, she reviews strategies for figuring out words by asking students what they should do when they come to a word they don't know. Students offer, "Sound it out; point with my finger." Since it is early in the year and students have not yet mastered looking at every letter in a word to decode it, Celia coaches by talking about partial decoding, "Do you ever look at the beginning letter and think about the story?" She reminds students to keep their eyes on her copy of the story and begins to read and model word-recognition strategies for the students. She models blanket by giving the beginning sounds for /bl/ and thinking aloud about the story: "*Pink bl. . . . Blanket.* I remember there was a pink blanket in the story. I like the way your eyes are up here." She models how to sound out "patches" by looking for a chunk. "I see a chunk *pat, ch* says /ch/, /es/, /patches/ does that make sense?" The students say, "Yes." She reads and makes a mistake, "Mama tried to hid the blanket. That doesn't sound right. I can try another sound for *i.*" She gives the long *i* sound and comes up with *hide.* "Let's go back and reread, Mama tried to hide the blanket." That makes sense." She also models how to sound out *dress* by using sequential decoding, /dr/ + /e/ + /s/, /dress/.

Day 1, Step 3: Coaching for Comprehension

(5 min.)

After reading aloud the story twice, with a focus on decoding strategies, now have students attune to the meaning of the story by asking a high-level question. What is a high-level question? It's one that that gets the children to think about the story. It's not answered with a *yes* or a *no*. The question may prompt students to connect the meaning of the story to their own lives. We have to expect our first graders to think—and to be capable of this level of response to texts. The payoff is worth it: Teachers who ask students to respond to higher-level questions about what they have read see greater growth in students' reading scores than teachers who do less of this type of questioning (Taylor et al. 2003, 2005). To ensure that each child understands the story sufficiently to participate in the higher-level thinking, take the time to briefly discuss the meanings of potentially unfamiliar but high-utility words not discussed in Step 2.

Coaching for Comprehension: Tips for Success

The purpose of coaching for comprehension is to *expand* students' comprehension of what they have read—rather than assess it. Higher-level questions are engaging, challenging, and require students to pause and think before answering. When coaching, you might:

▶ Ask children to summarize all or part of the story.

▶ Stretch children's understanding of the story by asking them interpretive questions.

▶ Invite children to determine a big idea of the story, or theme.

▶ Ask children to relate the story to their own lives.

Coaching for Comprehension:
Questions and Prompts for Teachers

During EIR lessons, the teacher questions and prompts children to expand their comprehension of and appreciation for what they just read. You want to pose questions that challenge students to pause and think before answering, that go beyond yes or no responses or factual information. Higher-level questions ask students to interpret a story and focus on a big idea, and get students to make connections between a text and their own experiences or with events in the world about them (Taylor et al. 2003).

Through Your Questioning, Students:

▶ Summarize all or part of the story.
▶ Stretch their understanding of the story.
▶ Relate the story to their life.
▶ Discuss a big idea or theme of the story.

Examples of Questions to Coach for Comprehension

▶ Summarize the story. What happened at the beginning of the story? the middle? the end? (Answer in just a few sentences.)
▶ How are you like Character X? How are you different?
▶ Why did Character X do Y?
▶ How did Character X change?
▶ What did you learn from this story?
▶ What did you like or not like about this story? Why?

Interpretive Questions Based on the Text

▶ What kind of person do you think (name of character) is? What in the story makes you think this?
▶ What are some good/bad things that happen in the story? Why do you think these are good/bad things?

▶ What do you think is an important thing that happened in the story? Why do you think it is important?
▶ How does (character in the story) compare to you or a family member? How is the character different?
▶ Why do you think the author gave the title he/she did to the story?
▶ What did you like best about (name a character)? Why? What in the story helped you think this way?
▶ What did you not like about (name a character)? Why? What in the story made you think this way?
▶ If you were the main character, would you have done the same things the main character did? Why or why not? What might you have done differently?
▶ Why do you think (character in the story) did . . . ?
▶ How did (character in the story) change? Why do you think this happened?
▶ What do you think were three main ideas (or most important ideas) in this article (for nonfiction)?

Higher-Level Questions Relating a Story Concept to Children's Lives

▶ Which character is most like you? Why?
▶ Which character would you like to be like? Why?
▶ Which character would you like to have as a friend? What in the story helped you make this decision?
▶ How are you like (character in the story)? How are you different?
▶ Can you compare anything in this story to (name another story or something else you have done in your classroom that could be compared)? Why do you think these are similar (alike) or different?
▶ Nonfiction type questions could relate to your state. (e.g., Could you find these animals, events in Minnesota? Why or why not? Where might they happen if they could be in Minnesota?).
▶ What did you like about this story? Why?

Figure 3-2 Coaching for Comprehension: Questions and Prompts for Teachers

Examples of questions to coach for comprehension include:

- What happened at the beginning of the story? The middle? The end? (Answer in just a few sentences.)

- Why did Character X do Y?

- How did Character X change?

- How are you like Character X? How are you different?

- What is this story really about?

- What did you learn from this story?

- What did you like about this story?

A variety of coaching for comprehension questions are found in Figure 3-2. You may want to print out the comprehension questions in Figure 3-2 and place them in your planning notebook or binder for easy access and reference. Also, on the DVD, there are vocabulary words and comprehension questions for exemplar books at different EIR reading levels. (See Appendices 4-2 and 4-3.)

☑ tips

EIR lessons are taught within a tight time frame; therefore, you will not have time for all students to answer your question. Let one or two children answer, and explain to the others that you will call on them on Day 2 or Day 3. I know this may depart from how you would normally have several children respond, but trust me that the children adapt well to it. Keep reminding yourself that wait time is important when asking children to express their thoughts. Wait at least 4 seconds after asking your question.

See it in Action

video
4

Coaching for Comprehension

After reading the new story, Celia asks students a high-level question, or one that a student has to pause and think about, as well as come up with his own idea before answering, such as "What did you like about the story and why?" She coaches for comprehension by asking students to elaborate on their ideas. Jake answers, "I liked when she got Rosa." Celia asks, "Why?" Jake says he forgot. Celia is patient and offers support. "Did Rosa help Geraldine?" Jake thinks for a moment and says, "Yes, the blanket got turned into a dress for her." Celia helps Jake make a connection to the story by asking him if he would like a new toy like Rosa. Jake answers, "Yes, but not that, a hockey toy."

Day 1, Step 4: Phonemic Awareness and Phonics Work (Sound Box Activity and Making Words)

(5 min.)

The Sound Box Activity

This activity is the fourth step on Day 1 and is used from October through December in first grade. (Starting in December or January, the children will switch to doing the Making Words activity instead of the Sound Box activity.)

During this final five minutes of the EIR lesson, children complete sound boxes on three to five words from the story. For examples of words to use in sound boxes with exemplar books, see the DVD Appendix 4-4. Have the children write the letter or letters for one sound per box. This helps them focus on hearing the sounds in words and develops their phonemic awareness. As students gain skill with this activity, you should do less of the exaggerating of sounds for them and let them do this on their own, as needed. They are often more successful if they say the actual words themselves.

You may also want to ask them how many sounds they hear in a word, which will tell them how many boxes they will be using. To help students become more independent, regularly use a short vowel chart in which the vowels and pictures starting with each short vowel sound are displayed, such as *a—apple, e—elephant, i—insect, o—octopus, u—umbrella* (see an example in Figure 3-3).

After writing the words in boxes, children should touch the words with their finger as they reread them. This helps them make the transition from hearing the sounds in words and writing the letters for these sounds to reading the words.

Figure 3-4 shows how the words that would be good choices to use when reading *Things I Like* by Anthony Browne (1989) would be inserted in the sound boxes. In *with,* the *th* goes together because these letters make just one sound. If a child can't tell what vowel is at the beginning of *in*, point to the short vowel chart and ask, "Is it the sound you hear at the beginning of *apple*? Is it the sound you hear at the beginning of *elephant*? *insect*? *octopus*? *umbrella*?"

The words that are best for sound boxes depend on the children's level of development and what you are stressing in your regular reading program. For the most part, you should select words made up of two to four phonemes that have phonetically regular long and or short vowel sounds represented by the CV, CVC, CVCC, or CVCE pattern (e.g., *go, hen, went, time* from *Rosie's Walk* by Pat Hutchins, 1968). Once children are gaining skill in hearing the phonemes in words, you may want to add initial consonant blends (e.g., *pl, br*) or digraphs (e.g., *sh, ch, th*).

Short Vowel Chart

Aa Ee Ii

Oo Uu

See the DVD for full-size versions of these forms.

Figure 3-3 *Short Vowel Chart*

Sound Boxes for *Things I Like* by Anthony Browne

1.	i	n		
2.	w	i	th	
3.	b	a	th	
4.	a	n	d	
5.	s	a	n	d

Figure 3-4 *Sound Boxes for* Things I Like *by Anthony Brown*

see it iN ActioN

Sound Boxes

Celia Huxley hands out sound box sheets to the five students in her EIR group. As they start with the first word, she says, "Listen carefully. Your job is to hear the sounds the words make and write the letters for them in the boxes. *Had*. What letter has the /h/ sound?" The students say *h*. Celia continues, "Write that down in the first box. What do you hear in the middle, /haaad/?" Students reply /a/. "Write *a* in the second box. What do you hear at the end? /had/?" Students say /d/. "Put your pencils down. Touch the letters like I do as we say the word. /h/, /a/, /d/, /had/." On the next word, *but*, Celia reminds the students to say the word before they start writing. When the students give the letter name *u* for /u/, she reminds them about the short vowel chart. "/U/ sounds like the *u* in *umbrella*. At the end of the word, they again reread it like they did with the first word, touching each letter as they say the sound for the letter, and then blending the sound together: /b/, /u/, /t/, /but/. Celia asks someone to use *but* in a sentence. Akouma says, "I have a blanket, but my mom washed it." When they come to the word *made* and Celia mentions the silent *e*, Jake shouts out that he has a silent *e* in his name. Celia praises him and tells them all to put the *e* with the *d* in the third box because they are putting one sound in a box and *e* is silent so it does not have its own box. When they come to the word *dress*, Celia helps the students with the double *s* at the end of the word. "You don't hear it, but sometimes words have two *s*'s at the end of the word." With Celia, the students read all five words on their chart, sound by sound, and then they blend the sounds together. "You did an outstanding job. Give yourselves a hug." She tells the students to take their sound box sheets home, read the words to Mom or Dad, and make up a sentence for each word just like they did for the word *but*.

 **tips**

As with the Sound Box activity, a good strategy with Making Words to help the children be successful is to have them say the words they are making. This is especially important for those who are still struggling with phonemic awareness. In first grade, especially at first, you should have the children spell a word that is close to the "mystery word" on their word before the "mystery word" boxes itself to avoid making the task too difficult.

Making Words

After two or three months of working with the sound boxes, Step 4 in Day 1 shifts to the Making Words activity to meet students' growing phonics knowledge. In Making Words, based on the work of Pat Cunningham (2009), children are given letter squares that spell a "mystery word" from the story. The teacher tells them to take two or three letters to start with and to make a particular word.

Then the teacher tells them to add a letter, perhaps take away a letter, or perhaps rearrange letters to spell a different word. At the end, the children are to use all of their letters to come up with a "mystery word" from the story. See the following example for how this activity might work. For examples of words to use in making words with exemplar books, see the DVD Appendix 4-5.

see it iN ActioN

Making Words

Celia Huxley has students put the letters *a, e, b, t, l, n,* and *k* in a row. (She has the set of letters ready to go in an envelope for each child.) "We are going to make some words using letters," she tells them. She explains how they will be playing a game that will help them be better readers. "The first word has three letters. Take three letters and make the word, *let.* /l/, /e/, /t/. What sound do you hear for the first letter?" Students say /l/. "What do you hear next? /l/, /e/, /t/?" Students say /e/. "What letter is this?" "What do you hear at the end?" Students say /t/. "What letter is this? Change one letter and make the word *net.* Now still use the same three letters and move them around to make the word *ten.* You say it. Everyone did it! Good job. Now take two letters and make the word *an.* Add two letters and make the word *tank.* What sound do you hear first? Listen carefully. Change one letter and make it say *bank.* How many letters do you have left? The next word is going to have seven letters. Can anyone figure out the secret word form the story about Geraldine?" A few students say, *"Blanket."* Most students have trouble spelling this word with their squares, so Celia coaches them individually. All are very interested in and intent on the task.

MAKING WORDS SEQUENCES FOR *BOATS* BY ANNE ROCKWELL

Hand out the following letter cards: *a, o, b, s, t* to each child.

Have students make the following words: *at, sat, bat, tab, stab, boats.* Say, "Take two letters and make the word *at.* Change one letter and make the word *sat.* Change one letter and make the word *bat.* Rearrange the letters you have to make the word *tab.* A tab is what you see on the edge of a folder [show a folder with a tab to the students]. Add one letter and make the word *stab.* Your dad might *stab* the steak to get it off the grill." At the end of the activity, say, "Now take all of the letters to make the mystery word from the story [*boats*]."

Sorting Words as Part of Making Words

After children have made words, it is important to show them cards that contain all of these words. You want students, one at a time, to tell you what words go together, whether this is by first letter or phonogram or by some other pattern. Often children like to see if the others can guess how they sorted their words. It is important to teach children how to sort by common phonograms and to talk about transfer to reading on their own. Regularly remind them that they may be able to figure out a hard word in the future by recognizing the phonogram, or word chunk, such as *–ab* in *stab*. For the exemplar book *Boats* by Anne Rockwell (example used on the previous page), students would hopefully come up with *at, sat,* and *bat* for one word sort and *tab* and *stab* for another.

The word sorts are an essential part of Making Words that often gets overlooked. You especially want the children to sort words by common phonograms. It is important to explain to the children, like Celia did in the *See It in Action* for Video 7, that learning to recognize common patterns, chunks, or phonograms will help them decode many words when they are reading on their own. I consistently recommend that teachers be explicit about students' transfer of strategies to independent reading in this way. In this case, Celia is reminding the children that they can look for these patterns in all the books they read.

Remember, you do not need to use the same exemplar books, but I hope the vocabulary, comprehension, and word work suggestions for these books give you ideas about the vocabulary to focus on, questions to ask, and words to use in word work in the books you do use.

See it in Action

video 7

Sorting Words

Celia puts word cards on a pocket chart. The words are the ones the children just made during the Making Words activity: *let, ten, net, an, tan, bank, tank, blanket.* "I'm going to show you one of the words. What does this word say?" Students say *ten* and Celia coaches them to come up with *net.* "What else could go with *net?* It rhymes with *net* and had the same ending *e, t.*" Students come up with *let.* Celia explains, "Good readers read lots of rhyming words. If you recognize the rhymes and know the patterns, you can read lots of words." Students come up with *tan* and *an* as words that go together, and *bank* and *tank* that go together. Celia asks, "Does anyone see another word with this pattern, /ank/?" She has to show them the /ank/ in *blanket.* She ends by talking again about transfer to reading. "If you see the pattern we have worked on, you'll be able to read lots of words when you are reading new books."

Summary of Day 1

As you can see, the four teaching steps for Day 1 are fairly straightforward. Nevertheless, you may want to reread the chapter and replay the video clips before you actually begin to teach Day 1. Also, after you have started to teach EIR lessons, by rereading the chapter, reviewing the videos, and discussing procedures with colleagues who are using EIR, you may come across points that you did not notice on your first reading that will help you be even more effective in your teaching. In the next sections of this chapter, I cover the procedures for Days 2 and 3 of the three-day cycle.

Preparing Making Words Sequences

- Start with words that follow the CVC or CVCe pattern at Level B. (See description of EIR reading levels in Table 4-1.)

- End with the second-to-the-last word that is close in spelling to the mystery word, especially at Level B (e.g., *pig, piglet*).

- You can move into some sequences with vowel combinations if you feel your students are ready for this at Level C.

- For reinforcement, try to pick phonics elements that are being taught in your regular reading program at a similar point in time.

- As you are doing a Making Words sequence, notice from the examples, that you typically should only change one letter each time.

- It is also a good idea, on occasion, to simply change the order of the letters, especially at Level B, so you can talk about how the order of the letters makes a difference (e.g., *was* vs. *saw*).

- Also, as you are preparing the Making Words sequences across stories, keep in mind that you want a variety of phonograms represented as opposed to using the same word family too often. For example, it would be better to select a mystery word for one story that features the *–at* word family, and for a second story to select a mystery word that features the *–ot* word family or two different CVE patterns than to select two stories that both feature the *–at* word family.

- While repetition is fine, it is also important to expose children to many different word families. I mention this because I realize how much I think about this as I select mystery words for different stories. Selecting a good mystery word, one that gives you a number of words and novel phonograms to make at students' reading level, isn't that easy.

Just as on Day 1, Day 2 has the same four components. You continue to work on the essential skills of word recognition, fluency, vocabulary, and comprehension, but you either focus on different students or you have a different emphasis in your teaching on one of the steps. In Step 1, as students reread old stories, they build their fluency and confidence as readers. You also get the chance to take a second oral reading check or coach a different student than you did the day before. As you reread the newest story in Step 2, you provide less support than you did on Day 1, because now, students have some familiarity with reading the story. As you do less of the work for the students, they do more, and they build their confidence as readers. In Step 3, you ask a second question about the story that gets the children thinking and you call on different students than you did the previous day for their answers. In Step 4, you continue to build word-recognition abilities by having students engage in a different activity. This time, they write a sentence instead of doing the Sound Boxes or Making Words activities.

Overview of the Lesson Steps

1. Group members reread stories from previous EIR lessons for fluency. Teacher conducts oral reading check or coaches in word recognition.

2. Group rereads "new" story twice while the teacher coaches as needed.

3. Teacher coaches for comprehension.

4. Students write a sentence about the story and teacher helps as needed. Each child should be engaged in hearing the sounds in the words and in trying to write the letters for these sounds. They should not be simply copying a sentence as the teacher writes it.

Day 2, Step 1: Reread EIR Stories

(5 min.)

As you did on Day 1, the first step in the Day 2 routine is to have the children reread "old" stories by themselves or with a partner. During this time, you should conduct an oral reading check or coach a child who is having trouble.

As you coach students, remind them to use a variety of different prompts such as:

▶ Sound it out letter by letter.

▶ Can you find a chunk or pattern you know?

▶ Think about what would make sense.

Day 2, Step 2: Read Newest Story

(5 min.)

Just as in Day 1, the next step in the routine is to have the children reread the "new" story twice. During the first reading, you may want to read the story as a choral reading, but now it's important that you let the children be the leading voice. That is, be sure you are saying the words *after* the children have said them. Also, continue to track for them on the first reading until they are able to track for themselves (at which time you would quit doing this altogether) and have them try to track on the second reading. At first, they will be unable to do this, but by consistently asking them to track and by coaching as needed, teachers find *that most grade 1 children in EIR are able to track by Thanksgiving.*

Second Reading

The second time through you may have the children read to a partner, to themselves, or by taking turns. If possible, have them read from their own copy of the story the second time through. If they are reading on their own or with a partner, you can listen to and coach individuals. If they are reading chorally or by turn taking, you also need to coach as children get stuck on words.

It is important to use a variety of prompts as you are coaching. Coaching prompts include questions that get the children to reflect on what they are doing (self-monitoring prompts) as well as questions that get them to try one or more word-attack strategies (decoding prompts). Examples of prompts are on page 38.

Remember, early in first grade, children in these EIR groups cannot independently decode by onset and rime. They must first grasp the alphabetic principle and will start to decode using the sound for the beginning letter and then they will use sequential decoding, which is letter-by-letter decoding. However, you should regularly model and coach students on decoding by onset and rime for first-grade students in the fall so it will be a familiar strategy they will try on their own later on.

You may want to make a Self-monitoring and Decoding Prompts chart to hang in the classroom so all students can refer to the prompts as they partner read.

Sometimes teachers tend to stress the same prompt, such as, "Sound it out," but this doesn't communicate to the children that there are multiple things they can try to figure out a word they don't know. Also, if a child pauses on a word and gets the word right or if the child self-corrects a word, you can praise the child and ask the child to explain what he did to figure out the word. By doing this, you are asking children to become aware of their metacognitive and self-monitoring efforts.

ʃee it iN ActioN

DAY 2
Rereading Newest Story

Students chorally read the "newest" story and track as they read. All students' eyes are intently fixed on the words on the pages as they are reading (glued to the print), a good sign that they are catching on to the reading they are doing. Next, students read with a partner as Celia listens to one student read. "I think you can handle this reading on your own. One reads one page and then the other person reads the next. Be sure you track as you read." Celia coaches one student who reads quite well. She also has to attend to others in the group to remind them to take turns reading with their partner and to track.

Day 2, Step 3: Coaching for Comprehension

(5 min.)

Just as you did on Day 1, with this next step you ask a higher-level question about the story and coach for comprehension. Since not everyone can answer every day, be sure to call on children you didn't call on during Day 1.

In the next example, Celia continues with questions to get Jake to say more about how he was like the character in the story. The fact that it is hard for children to express their thoughts tells me not that these types of questions are too hard but that we need to work on them more often.

ʃee it iN ActioN

Coaching for Comprehension

Celia says, "Think about Geraldine and the things she did in the story and think about the way she felt in the story. How are you like Geraldine?" Jake answers, "I have a blanket, but it is orange, and someone stepped on it and ripped it." Celia coaches him to elaborate, "How is this like Geraldine?" Jake says, "I take it everywhere."

Day 2, Step 4: Sentence Writing

(5 min.)

The fourth step on Day 2 is sentence writing, which helps students develop their spelling and reading skills. Usually, you ask the children for ideas, and then skillfully, but quickly, come up with a sentence for the group to write from the children's ideas. Each child should try to write the sentence himself, saying each word, listening for the sounds in sequence, and writing letters that go with these sounds. You can also write, but try to be a step behind the children so they don't simply copy you.

Consider the sentence, "The bus went across the town," that students might write after reading *School Bus* by Donald Crews. Although we want the children to do as much of the writing themselves as possible, if there are sounds that the children won't know how to spell, such as the /a/ and /o/ in *across* or the /ow/ in *town*, you should simply tell the children the letters for these sounds.

If children get stuck on a short vowel sound (that is spelled with a single letter), don't just tell them the letter but instead, help them learn to use the short vowel chart shown earlier to figure out how to spell a word with a particular short vowel sound. For example, help them figure out that the second sound in *bus* is the sound that is heard at the beginning of *umbrella*. It is important to keep the short vowel chart with you as you teach. Also, it is helpful to have an alphabet card at the table in case a child forgets how to write a particular letter.

Since the purpose of sentence writing is to develop children's phonemic awareness, phonics knowledge, and reading ability, and since they will be rereading their sentences at school or at home, I recommend that you have the children write words with the correct spelling. This is relatively easy to do when you are all writing the same sentence. At other times during the day when children are writing on their own, they will probably be writing with approximate spellings.

see it in Action

Sentence Writing

Celia says to her group, "We are going to write a sentence. Today I'm going to choose a sentence. Sometimes you choose, but we got a late start today. Tomorrow you get to choose." She gives them the sentence, *"Mama tried to hide the blanket.* What sound do you hear first? Mmmaaama." Students quickly come up with the letters for these sounds, *m* and *a*, and then *m* and *a*. "Leave a finger space. Eyes up here. Look at me. Tried, trrried, triiied." Students come up with *tr* and *i*. Celia says "Tried," and Jake quickly comes up with *d."* Celia says, "You can't hear the *e*, so I'm going to tell you. There is an *e* before the *d*. Students quickly come up with the spelling for *to* and *the.* Celia says, "You know your word wall words." Students also know there is a silent *e* on the end of *hide.* Celia has to coach students on writing *blanket.* Akouma says *bal* for *bl.* Celia has them say *blanket* to help them hear the sounds in the correct order. She asks them if they can remember the pattern *-ank* they worked on, and Nick quickly comes up with *a, n, k.* Celia coaches them on the *e* before the *t,* saying that it is hard to hear. Students reread their sentence twice, pointing to the words they have written as they read. Celia ends with, "Give yourselves a big clap."

✓ tips

Helpful Resources on the DVD
Remember, for exemplar EIR books, vocabulary to focus upon, questions to use when coaching for comprehension, words to use in sound boxes and sentence writing, words for making words activities are provided full size on the DVD so you can print them out as needed if you are using any of these books.

Summary of Day 2

Day 2 reinforces and deepens students' understandings from Day 1 by increasing their fluency with repeated readings, extending their word recognition through additional opportunities to read with the teacher, as well as expanding their comprehension with further comprehension questions and sentence writing.

Day 3
Lesson Routine

The Day 3 routine is almost the same as the Day 2 routine. The biggest difference you'll notice is that your students will be able to contribute with greater independence now, because the three-day routine provides a gradual release of responsibility to the students. The practice and consistent structure, plus the additional small-group work with you, combine to help children feel more confident and capable as independent readers.

Overview of the Lesson Steps

1. Group members reread any stories from previous EIR lessons for fluency. Teacher conducts oral reading check or coaches in word recognition.

2. Group rereads "new" story twice while the teacher coaches as needed.

3. Teacher coaches for comprehension.

4. Group writes a second sentence about the story and teacher provides support as needed. Each child should be engaged in hearing the sounds in the words and in trying to write the letters for these sounds. A child should not be simply copying a sentence as the teacher writes it.

Day 3, Step 1: Reread Old Stories

(5 min.)

As you did on Days 1 and 2, begin the routine by having children reread "old" stories by themselves or with a partner as you conduct an oral reading check or coach a child who is struggling. Of course, it is important to get around to all of the children and coach as they read, but you will find that since there are numerous opportunities for coaching built into the EIR model, you can especially focus on those children who are most in need of your help in Step 1 of Day 3.

ʃee it iN ActioN

DAY 3
Rereading Old Stories

Celia starts out by saying, "We're going to read a story we've read before. I'm going to listen to Shaun as Jake and Akouma are partners and Andy and Nick are partners. What do good readers do when they come to a word they don't know?" The children offer, "Track, sound them out. Look at the first letter." Celia coaches by asking them if they ever read on and come back to a word they don't know, and the children say they do. Celia also reminds the children not to blurt out a word if their partner gets stuck, but to instead give their partner a clue. She coaches as Shaun reads but also frequently monitors the other students' progress with partner reading.

Day 3, Step 2: Read Newest Story

(5 min.)

The second step of the Day 3 routine is to have the children reread the newest story twice—the story they have been reading for the past two days. By Day 3, students should be reading the story from their own copy (not reading from your copy as you track). You may have the children read to a partner, to themselves, or by taking turns. As children are reading on their own or with a partner, you can listen to and coach individuals. If they need help with short vowel sounds, have them use the short vowel chart (Figure 3-3 on page 45).

As children read with a partner, it is important to remind them not to shout out a word when a partner gets stuck, but to instead give a hint. We have found it helpful to give children a few things to say when a partner gets stuck. They will need constant, gentle reminding, however, to use the prompts (see student prompts on page 38).

ʃee it iN ActioN

video
12

Partner Reading

Celia says, "Today we are going to read Geraldine again. This is our last day on this story. First you will read to me, and then partner read." Students take turns reading for the teacher. Celia compliments them by saying, "You are such good readers!" When Jake reads, she coaches him on made. He says *mad*. "Try the other sound /ay/." Jake slowly comes up with *made*. Celia then has students partner read and she reads with Jake who had the most trouble reading the story. She reminds students to help their partner if he or she gets stuck. She coaches Jake who reads *couldn't* for *could not*. He pauses on *make* but decodes it correct on the first try this time. When Jake reads *they* for *there*, Celia coaches, "Let's look at this word. How do you know it can't say *they?*" Jake says, "Because it does not have an *ey.*" He sounds out *there*. Celia praises Jake for his reading, "I like how you corrected words yourself."

Day 3, Step 3: Coaching for Comprehension

(5 min.)

Now that students have in a sense warmed up with fluency practice, turn your attention to making sure they understand what they are reading. Again, ask one question about the story that gets the children thinking, or ask about how the children's lives are related to the story. Since not everyone can answer every day, be sure to call on children you didn't call on during Days 1 or 2.

See it iN Action

video
13

Coaching for Comprehension

Celia tells students that she is going to ask them a hard question and they will really have to think. "Think about Geraldine in the whole story. How did she change? How did she feel?" The children have a hard time so Celia coaches, "How did Geraldine feel at the beginning?" The children say she felt happy. "How did she feel in the middle?" The children say sad, and Celia coaches for elaboration. "What made her sad?" Akouma says, "She had to give away her blanket." "How did she feel at the end?" Celia asks. The children say she felt happy. Celia summarizes, "She made a lot of changes."

Day 3, Step 4: Sentence Writing

(5 min.)

The fourth step, as in Day 2, is sentence writing. In the fall in first grade, the students continue to write a group sentence. It is important that each child try to write the group sentence on their own, saying each word, listening for the sounds in sequence, and writing letters that go with these sounds. As the year progresses, the teacher will help less as the children are writing. For example, by November or December, the children will not need to all be on the same word at the same time.

However, by late winter or early spring, depending on the children's ability, they should be able to write individual sentences. The teacher gives the group a prompt and each child writes her own sentence in response to this prompt. The child uses approximate, or invented, spelling. Once children finish their sentence, they share it with the teacher. She does not correct all misspelled words but helps each child with one or two words to refine the child's phonemic awareness.

ʃee it iN ActioN

video
14

Sentence Writing: Fall

Celia lets students come up with their own sentence on Day 3. Students offer sentences, *"Geraldine got a pink blanket." "Mama tried to hide the blanket." "Geraldine had a new doll."* Celia moves things along by saying, "Let's write the one Nick said and next time I'll choose someone else's sentence." Nick repeats his sentence, *"Geraldine got a pink blanket."* Celia coaches, "Geraldine, say the first sound /j/. It is the letter *g* this time, not the letter *j*." She has them say the word as they write it. She gives them the *e*, but asks them to come up with the *r*, helps them with the *a* but asks them to come up with the *l* and *d*, gives them the *i* since it is not *e*. One of the students knows there is an *e* at the end of the word. Students write *got, a, pink* with coaching support from their teacher. For the word *got*, she stops to briefly talk about the fact that the g in *Geraldine* says /j/ and the *g* in *got* says /g/. When they come to *blanket*, she says, "This is a hard one, but you can do it! Remember the /ank/ from Making Words. You are doing so well!" She has them put their pencils down

and they track as they reread the sentence they have just written. Students' eyes are closely "glued" to the print, a good sign that they are catching on to the reading of what they have just written.

ſee it iN ActioN

Sentence Writing: Winter

In the second example, Celia moves quickly by coming up with a sentence related to an idea the students had the day before. She has students repeat the words in the sentence they are writing, which helps them to hear the sound in the words as they write them. She also does a minilesson on words often ending in *ll* instead of *l*.

Celia begins by saying, "Yesterday you told me that you like it when the troll fell in the water. So today, we are going to write, *The troll fell into the water.* Let's all say it." She coaches as students write. Shaun has written *toll* for *troll*. "What comes after the *t*?" Shaun adds an *r*. Celia coaches the group, "You are all doing really well, but let's check our work. You wrote all the letters you heard in *troll*, but there are two *l*'s. You can't tell, so I'll just give you the second *l*." She uses the short vowel chart when Shaun has trouble with the right letter for the vowel sound in *tell*. She tells students to write the last three words on their own, and coaches some on the *e* in /er/. "I'm so impressed. You really are great writers."

Sentence Writing Late Winter/Early Spring

In the spring, Celia does not give students a group sentence to write. She either gives them a prompt or tells them to come up with their own sentence about the story and reminds them not to copy from the book. She coaches students as they are writing. When students finish their sentence, they read it to the teacher and she coaches them on one or two words in which sounds for a word are not represented with letters or the letters for sounds in a word are in the wrong order.

Daily Opportunity for One-on-One Reading Practice with a Coach

(5–7 min. beyond the EIR lesson)

In addition to working with the teacher daily in a small group, each child also needs the opportunity every day to reread their current EIR story (or an older EIR story if they have not yet read the newest story with the teacher) to someone. That someone might be an educational assistant, a parent, or an older student who has been trained to coach. This is an essential part of this intervention that often gets overlooked. It may be difficult to find people to do the one-on-one coaching, but children's progress is rapid when this important piece is in place. If adults are not available to do the one-on-one coaching, we have found that children a few years older than the first graders can be taught to do an effective job of coaching (Taylor et al. 1997). Teachers have found that this cross-age tutoring (described in the Grade 3 and Grade 4/5 versions of *Catching Readers*) not only helps the younger students improve in reading, but it also helps the third, fourth, or fifth graders improve in reading, particularly in their concepts about themselves as readers.

tips

As I emphasize the value of one-on-one coaching using volunteers, I want to stress the point that I do not believe the EIR small-group lesson should be taught by anyone but a licensed teacher. Children who are having trouble learning to read need extra quality instruction from those who have the most expertise.

It should only take about five to seven minutes for a child to read an EIR story to a coach. A coach needs to know how to give support on easier words in lieu of just telling students words when they get stuck. On the other hand, a coach also needs to know when to simply provide hard words if children are getting frustrated or if the words are longer words that cannot be readily decoded by most first graders. In Chapter 8, I provide suggestions for the training of one-on-one coaches.

Summary of Day 3

As you can see, the four teaching steps for Days 1, 2, and 3 build on one another to strengthen students' confidence and abilities as they learn to read. By March or earlier, many first graders are ready to read books with less scaffolding and teacher support. This phase of EIR is called the *transition phase*, and I'll describe it in more detail in Chapter 5. The routine changes slightly but the same elements regarding word recognition, fluency, and comprehension remain in place, only now students are more independent.

Next, let's look at the kinds of books you'll be using, as well as reproducibles that you can use so that you, your coaches, and parents are ready to help first graders become readers.

Book Selection Guides and Other Lesson-Planning Resources

Providing students with quality children's literature to read is an essential piece of effective instruction, and every EIR lesson relies on an engaging book. Too often struggling readers are given materials that hinder their achievement—dull texts written to drill skills rather than engage young readers in meaningful stories and nonfiction. In this chapter, I give you guidance on how to select the best books written by top-notch children's authors. However, I want to emphasize that you need to make your own choices and discoveries about the fiction and nonfiction books to use in EIR lessons. Why? Because following someone else's suggestions somehow flattens the vitality of the teaching and learning. Go with your own expertise and interests, as well as the curiosities and sense of humor of your students.

In this chapter, you will find charts that will help you know the characteristics to look for when choosing books for EIR as well as sample lists that will show how to use these books to plan and carry out the four lesson steps. You'll see lists on comprehension, vocabulary, phonics, and word sorting/making activities. Two valuable forms I want to highlight now are: The lesson planning template below (also found in Figure 4-1 and the sample reading at home

All the forms in this chapter are available on the DVD in full size.

Generic Lesson-Planning Form

Sound Box or Making Words	**Coaching for comprehension questions for Days 1, 2, and 3** (List the questions to ask children.)
Oral Reading Check results and notes for following children:	
Notes	
Take-Home Activity (Notes regarding Take-Home Activity)	

Figure 4-1 Generic Lesson-Planning Form

sheet (Figure 4-2). Both resources have a comforting structure that you'll get used to quickly. And don't forget the importance of encouraging parents/caregivers to instill good reading habits in their first graders!

Reading at Home Sheet

Date _____

_____ has read the book
(student's name)

_____ to me _____ times.
(book title)

Comments: _____

_____

_____

_____

_____

_____

_____

_____

_____
(parent's/caregiver's signature)

Figure 4-2 Reading at Home Sheet

Grade 1 Books: What to Look For

Books for grade 1 are divided into four levels that cover preprimer 1, preprimer 2–3, primer, and end of grade 1 levels. I call them EIR levels in this book so they aren't confused with Guided Reading Levels (Fountas and Pinnell 1996).

In first grade, you will need six to seven books at each of the EIR Levels A, B, C, and D (see Table 4-1). Examples of suitable books for the EIR model are shown in Table 4-2. Remember, you do not need to use these specific books, but I include them to give you an idea of the types of books that work well with the EIR model. In addition to quality children's literature, there are some leveled book series from major publishing houses that you can select texts from as well, including Step into Reading, All Aboard Reading, Early I Can Read, and others. The important thing is that students will find the books engaging so that they're motivated to do the hard work of learning to reading.

Characteristics of Grade 1 Books at Different EIR Levels

EIR Level	Traditional Reading Level	Guided Reading Level*	Length (words)	Time to Use
Level A	PP[1]	DE	40–60	Oct.–Nov.
Level B	PP[2–3]	FG	60–90	Dec.–Jan.
Level C	P	GH (small-group repeated reading)		
	PP–P	DEFG (transition)	90–120	Feb.–March
Level D	P–1[2]	HI (transition)	120–200	March–May

PP[1, 2, 3] = preprimer, levels 1, 2, 3, P = primer, 1[2] = end-of-first-grade reading level

*From Fountas and Pinnell (1996), Guided Reading. Portsmouth, NH: Heinemann.

Table 4-1 Characteristics of Grade 1 Books at Different EIR Levels

Teachers use the basic three-day routine as described in Chapter 3 with books at EIR Levels A and B, and half of the books at EIR Level C. The transition phase (see Chapter 5 and Figure 5-1) are used with half of the books at EIR Level C and all of the books at EIR Level D.

Whether you use children's literature or leveled books, do not select books that are highly predictable (e.g., children can read them with their eyes shut). Predictable books just don't work with this intervention model. The goal of EIR is to get children to glue to the print and to try to figure out the alphabetic principle as soon as possible; when the text has a repetitive pattern, students do not focus on the print as much as they should. For this reason, in the EIR model, books start at the guided reading level of D.

Examples of Grade 1 Books

EIR Level	Book Title	Author
A: 40–60 words, preprimer 1 level, use Oct.–Nov.	*Sam's Cookie* *Sam's Ball* *Things I Like* *Big Pig and Little Pig* *Bugs* *Splat!* *Jack and Rick* *Rick Is Sick*	Barbro Lindgren Barbro Lindgren Anthony Browne David McPhail Patricia and Fred McKissack Mary Margaret Perez-Mercado David McPhail David McPhail
B: 60–90 words, preprimer 2–3 level, use Dec.–Jan.	*School Bus* *Sleepy Bear* *Sheep in a Jeep* *Boats* *Big Brown Bear* *Rosie's Walk* *Across the Stream* *Thunder Doesn't Scare Me!* *I Love Rocks*	Donald Crews Lydia Dabcovich Nancy Shaw Anne Rockwell David McPhail Pat Hutchins Mirra Ginsburg Lynea Bowdish Cari Meister
C: 90–120 words, repeated reading, primer level, Feb.–March (Note, these books are harder than the C books below since students will be reading them repeatedly over the 3-day cycle.)	*Carrot Seed* *Hooray for Snail* *Rain* *Growing Vegetable Soup*	Ruth Krauss John Stadler Marion Dane Bauer Louise Ehlert
C: 90–120 words, transition, pre primer and primer levels, use Feb.–March (Note, these books are easier than the C books above since students will be reading them 'cold.")	*Cat Traps* *The Chick and the Duckling* *Herman the Helper* *Go Away, Dog*	Molly Coxe Mirra Ginsburg Robert Kraus Joan Nodset
D: 120–200 words, transition, primer and grade 1 levels, use March–May	*Good Night Owl* *The Happy Day* *Just for You* *All By Myself* *There's a Nightmare in My Closet* *You'll Soon Grow into Them, Titch* *Tiger Is a Scaredy Cat* *Kit and Kat* *Sleepy Dog*	Pat Hutchins Ruth Krauss Mercer Mayer Mercer Mayer Mercer Mayer Pat Hutchins Joan Phillips Tomie dePaola Harriet Ziefert

Also at Level D: easy reader series for beginning readers such as Step into Reading—Step 1, Random House; All Aboard Reading—Levels 1 and 2, Grosset & Dunlap; HarperCollins: Hello Reading, Viking; I Can Read Level 1; My First I Can Read.

Table 4-2 Examples of Grade 1 Books

GUIDELINES FOR SELECTING GRADE 1 EIR BOOKS

▌ **Reading selections should follow the length guidelines for EIR Levels A, B, C, and D that are in Table 4-1.** Transition books at Level C are easier than the group repeated reading books at Level C. If you want to use a book at a particular level but it is too long, have the children only read part of the selection over the three-day cycle and then read another part over a second three-day cycle.

▌ **Make sure a story is complex and interesting enough that you and the children can spend three days on it and still be engaged.** You need to be able to ask higher-level questions about the story for three days. I have found that many leveled readers may not be engaging enough to spend that much time on them, so you need to select them carefully.

▌ **At EIR Level A, you do not want a story to be so patterned and predictable that a child can read it "with his eyes shut."** In a story such as the following, children can "read" the text by looking at the pictures instead of the words: "One black dog runs, two white rabbits hop, three red birds sing, etc." Instead, in EIR lessons, we want children's eyes to "glue to the print."

▌ **At all levels, but especially with the transition books at Level C, there should be enough CVC words (e.g., consonant-vowel-consonant words) in texts that a child can practice letter-by-letter sequential decoding.** Also, you would not want a book that primarily used CVC words with only short *a*, for example (e.g., Pat is a cat. Pat sat on her hat. Pat's hat is flat.). A child needs to problem solve—what is the short *a* sound in this word? What is the short *i* sound in this word (e.g., Pat is a cat. Pat did tricks with a hat. We had fun with Pat the Cat)? See Table 4-3 for a suggested scope and sequence of phonic elements to stress in word work.

Scope and Sequence of Phonic Elements to Focus on in Word Work

Level A	Level B	Level C	Level D
short a	short e	sp	cl
short i	CVC-e	sl	pr
short u	ee	sw	dr
short o	ai	sn	sc
	ar		ch
	gr	th	wh
	gl	er	qu
	st	ay	ea
	cr	ing	oo
	sm	ir	ow
	br		ou
	fl		y = long i
	sh		
	ck		

Table 4-3 Scope and Sequence of Phonic Elements to Focus on in Sound Box and Making Word Activities

Book-Related Resources to Help You Plan Lessons

Remember, you do not need to use the particular books that are listed here. Use them as exemplars to get you started, along with the sample support material that follows. What is important is that you understand what phonic elements to focus upon with the leveled books you choose to use for EIR lessons. Additional resources that will help you teach EIR lessons are available on the DVD. Materials include teaching charts; take-home activities for the children (Appendix 4-1) ; a list of exemplar EIR books (also see Table 4-2); and for exemplar books, vocabulary to focus upon, questions to use when coaching for comprehension, words to use in word work, sound boxes, sentence writing, words for making words activities, and lesson planning forms and independent activities for exemplar transition books. (See Appendices 4-2 to 4-6). There are also assessment directions and recording forms (see Chapter 5). All of these materials are also provided full size on the DVD so you can print them out as needed.

See these additional forms on the DVD

Take-Home Activities/Level A

Title of the Story: _____   Parent Signature: _____

Student Name: _____

Choose words from the story. Write the word on the line and draw a picture of that word.

Choose your word.   Draw a picture.   Write it again.

Appendix 4-1 Generic Take-Home Activities

Examples of Vocabulary to Discuss in Exemplar Grade 1 Books

Please Note: These are only suggested words to talk about in terms of meaning at point of contact in the stories. Teachers should make choices based on their students' needs. I want to thank the elementary and ELL teachers who helped with these lists.

Books	Possibilities for All Students	Possibilities for ELLs
Level A		
Sam's Cookie		scared, angry
Sam's Ball		kitty, meow
Things I Like	acrobatics	wading, dreaming
Big Pig and Little Pig		pool, bucket
Bugs		hundred, skinny, everywhere
Splat!	splat, mistake	frosting
Jack and Rick		lift, pass
Rick Is Sick	brag	win, tired, miss, nap
Level B		
School Bus		empty
Boats	oars, paddles, barges, tugs	motors, engines
Big Brown Bear		paint, washes, windows, set
Rosie's Walk	mill, haystack, pond	beehives
Across the Stream		dream, stream kind, luck
Thunder Doesn't Scare Me		afraid, thunder, brave, parade, over, crawl
I Love Rocks	dams, slimy	jewels, pool
Level C		
Carrot Seed	sprinkled	planted, afraid
Rain	wilt, gather	heavy, tiny, fresh, puddle
Growing Vegetable Soup	sprouts	vegetable, soup, tools
Cat Traps	traps, chow	snack
The Chick and the Duckling	duckling, chick	worm, butterfly
Herman the Helper	enemies, poor, needy, mashed	policeman, fireman
Level D		
Just for You	groceries	lawn, crusts, special
All by Myself	overalls, trim	fur, bush
There's a Nightmare in My Closet	rid	nightmare, closet, afraid, safe
You'll Soon Grow	hit, big	
		brave, scared, sorry, vacuum cleaner
	lly, seesaw	stuff, surprise, pedals
		covers, pillows

Appendix 4-2 Examples of Vocabulary to Discuss in Exemplar Grade 1 Books

---

Examples of Questions for Exemplar Grade 1 Stories

Please note that these are only examples. If you are using some of these books, you may wish to come up with your own questions.

Level A

Sam's Cookie
▶ Who can tell us something interesting or funny about their dog or a dog they know?

Sam's Ball
▶ How is this cat like a cat you know? What are some funny things cats do?

Things I Like
▶ What is something that the chimp likes to do that you like to do? Tell why.

Big Pig and Little Pig
▶ Which pig did you think made a better pool and why?

Bugs
▶ Do you like bugs? If so, what kinds do you like and why? If not, what kinds don't you like and why?

Splat!
▶ Did you or someone in your family ever have a big mess in the kitchen? Tell about it.
▶ What do you think is the funniest part of this story and why?

Jack and Rick
▶ What does this story tell us about two friends helping one another?
▶ What part of this story do you like the best and why?

Rick Is Sick
What do you like to do when you are sick to make yourself feel better?

Level B

School Bus
▶ Who can tell us something interesting or funny about a bus ride to school or to somewhere else?

Sheep in a Jeep
▶ Can anyone tell us about a time they got stuck going somewhere? How did you get free?

Boats
▶ Who can tell us something interesting or funny about a time they were on a boat? Where were you? Who were you with? What did you do on the boat?

Big Brown Bear
▶ Who can tell us about a time they saw a bear? Where were you? What was the bear doing?

Rosie's Walk
▶ Who can tell us something interesting or funny about a time they were on a farm? Where were you? Who were you with? What did you do on the farm?

Across the Stream
▶ Who can tell us about seeing ducks in a pond or lake? Where were you? What did you see?

Thunder Doesn't Scare Me
▶ How do you feel about thunder? Does it scare you? Why or why not?

I Love Rocks
▶ Do you ever pick up rocks? If so, where? What do you do with the rocks you pick up? Do you put them down? Do you save them?

continues

Appendix 4-3 Examples of Questions for Exemplar Grade 1 Stories

Examples of Words to Use for Word Work, Sound Boxes, and Sentence Writing for Exemplar Grade 1 Books

Book	Introduction	Choices for Review	Words to Use for Word Work, Sound Box, and Sentence Writing
Level A			
Sam's Cookie		short a	Sam, has, Sam's
Sam's Ball	short a		Sam, has, bad, can, and
Things I Like	short i		this, is, with, kick, in
		short a	bath, and, sand
Big Pig and Little Pig	short o		hot
		short a	can
		short i	dig, big, pig, sit, fill
		short u	up
Bugs	short u		bugs, up
Splat!		short a	cat, dad, splat!
Jack and Rick		short a	can, pass
		short o	log
		short u	up
		short i	big, lift
Rick Is Sick		short i	Rick, sick, it's, is, sits
		short a	can, Jack, bag, has, nap
Level B			
School Bus	sm		
		short o	cross, stop, on
		short i	it, this
		short a	and, that
Sheep in a Jeep	ee		beep, sheep, weep, sweep, steep, jeep
	sh		shrug, sheep
	st		steer, steep
		short e	yelp, help, get
		short u	thud, tug, mud, shrug
Boats	ai		sails
	fl		float
		short o	on, ponds
		short i	it, sits, big, pig
Big Brown Bear		short u	up
		short i	is, big
		short a	bat, has
		short e	get, set, yet

Appendix 4-4 Examples of Words to Use for Word Work, Sound Boxes, and Sentence Writing for Exemplar Grade 1 Books

Examples of Making Words Sequences for Grade 1 Books

Level B

School Bus
a, e, l, r, t
tar
rat
rate
late
later

Sheep in a Jeep
a, h, l, p, s, s
pal
lap
sap
slap
[start over]*
ash
lash
splash

Boats
a, o, b, s, t
tab
bat
sat
stab
boats

Big Brown Bear
i, o, w, w, n, d, s
so
no
in
sin
win
wind
window
windows

Rosie's Walk
a, a, c, h, k, s, t, y
say
stay
hay
sack
tack
stack
haystack

Across the Stream
a, e, m, r, s, t
eat
meat
team
steam
stream

Thunder Doesn't Scare Me
u, e, n, t, h, d, r
net
ten
hen
den
nut
hut
thud
thunder

I Love Rocks
c, s, t, l, s, a, e
castles
cat
sat
set
let
last—Tell the children the vowel is changing so they need to listen carefully to the middle sounds.
cast
castle—Tell the children we write an *e* at the end when we spell this word even though we can't hear it.

*Students are to put all of their letters back in front of them and start from scratch to make a new word.

Appendix 4-5 Examples of Making Words Sequences for Exemplar Grade 1 Books

Lesson-Planning Forms and Independent Activities for Exemplar Transition Books

The Carrot Seed by Ruth Krauss

Making Words
o, u, d, g, n, r
on
no
nod
rod
round
ground

Coaching for Comprehension Que...
2, and 3
(List the questions to ask children...

Independent Activities (Optional)

Writing Prompts
1. If you were going to plant a seed, what kind would you plant? Why?
2. Why do you think the boy believed the seed would grow even though everyone told him it wouldn't?
Summary—Give students first sentence below (from the beginning).
1. The little boy planted a carrot seed and watered it every day.
2. (Write about what happens in the middle of the story.)
3. (Write a sentence about the end of the story.)

Word Families
Write other words that end like and rhyme with:

seed	ground
creed	pound
greed	hound
weed	bound
heed	found
need	round
speed	sound

Take-Home Activity
(Notes regarding take-home activity.)

Oral Reading Check/Oral Reading Analysis
(Completed for the children listed.)

Appendix 4-6 Lesson-Planning Forms and Independent Activities for Exemplar Transition Books

5

The Transition Phase

· ·

Helping First Graders Read Independently

Typically, by February or March in first grade, or earlier if students are ready, you'll shift to the transition phase of EIR. You base this shift on students' oral reading check scores (see Chapter 6) and, of course, your own knowledge of each young reader. The hallmark of this phase is that you're coaching children as they read a book *they have never read before* in an EIR lesson.

All year long, your first graders who are in EIR have been "reading" books independently at the emergent reading level (e.g., Guided Reading Levels A–C, Fountas and Pinnell 1996), looking at many other books in the room, and rereading books from their guided reading group lessons. Much of this independent reading transpires during the independent work time of the reading block. The difference now is that you bring independent reading of books students have never read before into the EIR lesson itself with books at a mid to end of first-grade level. Your goal is to get children reading independently for sustained periods as soon as possible on a solid first-grade level (e.g., Guided Reading Levels H–I). Once they can really read on their own, they need to practice reading as much as possible. Hopefully, they will then be reading on grade level by the end or the year.

The transition reading procedures that are detailed in this chapter and summarized in the box below and again in on the DVD are used with four transition books at EIR Level C and all of the books at EIR Level D in grade 1 (see box on next page for a list of exemplar books at these levels).

Transition Procedures for Level C and D Books in Grade 1
(February or March– May)

Read a Level C small-group book (such as one from the small-group list of exemplar books) following the regular three-day repeated reading format with the group of students.

▶ Then select a Grade 1 Level C transition book (such as one from the list of exemplar books to be used with the transition procedures.)

▶ Then go back to reading a Level C small-group book following the basic three-day repeated reading format with the group.

▶ The next three-day cycle select a Grade 1 Level C transition book to use with the transition procedures.

▶ Continue until all Level C books are completed.

▶ Grade 1 Level D: Use the transition process with all of the Level D books for the remainder of the school year.

When teachers use the transition books at Grade 1 Levels C/D, the procedures change as follows:

▶ The teacher works with two students at a time. She may not get to all pairs of students in three days.

▶ The teacher does not first read the book to the children. The teacher has the children read the book "cold" and provides the support each child needs. Children can take turns reading.

▶ The teacher continues to help with the use of phonics and contextual analysis as needed.

▶ The writing component can be continued if time permits.

▶ After the children have read with the teacher, the trained coach listens to the children, one at a time. The trained coach reinforces the children's efforts to sound out words and to use context to unlock meanings of unfamiliar words.

▶ Examples of independent activities for the other EIR children are provided on the lesson planners on the DVD. Also, the other children can reread old stories or read new ones independently or with a partner.

Figure 5-1   Transition Procedures for Level C and D Books in Grade 1 (February or March–May)

Exemplar Books at EIR Levels C and D

EIR Level	Book Title	Author
C: Small group, 90–120 words, repeated reading, primer level, Feb.–March (Note: these books are harder than the C books below since students will be reading them repeatedly over the three-day cycle.)	*Carrot Seed* *Hooray or Snail* *Rain* *Growing Vegetable Soup*	Ruth Krauss John Stadler Marion Dane Bauer Louise Ehlert
C: Pairs–transition, 90–120 words, pre-primer and primer levels, Feb.–March (Note: these books are easier than the C books above since students will be reading them "cold.")	*Cat Traps* *The Chick and the Duckling* *Herman the Helper* *Go Away, Dog*	Molly Coxe Mirra Ginsburg Robert Krauss Joan Nodset
D: Pairs–transition, 120–200 words, primer and grade 1 levels, March–May	*Good Night Owl* *The Happy Day* *Just for You* *All By Myself* *There's a Nightmare in My Closet* *You'll Soon Grow into Them, Titch* *Tiger Is a Scaredy Cat* *Kit and Kat* *Sleepy Dog*	Pat Hutchins Ruth Krauss Mercer Mayer Mercer Mayer Mercer Mayer Pat Hutchins Joan Phillips Tomie dePaola Harriet Ziefert

Also at Level D: Easy readers series for beginning readers such as Step into Reading—Step 1, Random House; All Aboard Reading—Levels 1 and 2, Grosset & Dunlap; Hello Reading, Viking; I Can Read Level 1; My First I Can Read, HarperCollins.

Table 5-1 Exemplar Books at EIR Levels C and D

When Are Students Ready?

In writing this book, I struggled with where to put the assessment chapter. I decided I wanted to give you all the lesson cycle routines before going into detail about which children benefit from EIR, the assessments involved, and how you know they're ready for the midyear transition. You can flip to the next chapter if you want to take a glance at the assessments, but for now two rules of thumb:

1. If students are able to read books they have never seen before that are at an early preprimer level (or Guided Reading Levels of D and E) with at least 92 percent accuracy in word recognition, they are ready to read the transition books at EIR Level C.

2. If your students are able to read books they have never read before that are at a late preprimer to primer level (or Guided Reading Levels of F–G) with at least 92 percent accuracy in word recognition, then they are ready to read transition books at EIR Level D (primer to end of first-grade level or Guided Reading Levels H–I) in EIR lessons.

IF YOU STARTED EIR MIDYEAR

If you started the intervention in February, you most likely began with the three-day repeated reading cycle with several EIR Level C books to build up students' confidence. However, if students are able to read books *they have never seen before* that are at a preprimer level or Guided Reading Levels of D and E with at least 92 percent accuracy in word recognition, they are ready to begin with the easier transition books at EIR Level C as well.

February–May: How the Three-Day Routine Changes

Now the EIR routine changes. The teacher rotates between teaching the three-day, 20-minute repeated reading cycle with Level C books to everyone and coaching pairs of students for 10 to 15 minutes per pair on a new Level C transition book across a three-day period. I know that's a lot to take in, so refer to the day-by-day reading rotation on the next page.

When the teacher is coaching pairs, she no longer works with all of the children in a group at once but instead reads with two children at a time. After she has read with them, they should reread their story to their partner, to themselves, and to their one-on-one coach. The other students in the EIR group reread favorite books, read new books, and complete open-ended response activities related to books they have read. (In Chapter 7, I describe a number of motivating independent activities for children as they are interacting with texts, and I offer open-ended response sheets for these activities as well.) Also, on the lesson planners for exemplar books on the DVD, there are useful independent activities children can work on while you work with other pairs in the EIR group.

Small-Group and Transition Reading Rotation Procedures

Days 1–3

Read a Level C book with first graders (such as a book from the small-group book list in Table 5-1). Use the regular three-day routine covered in Chapter 3 with the entire group of students.

Days 4–6

Now select a Grade 1 Level C from the Table 5-1 (such as a book from the pairs-transition list). Use the book with the transition reading steps described next.

Days 7–9

Now go back to reading a different Level C book (such as one from the small-group book list in Table 5-1), following the basic three-day repeated reading format with the group.

Days 10–12

For the next three-day cycle, select a Grade 1 Level C book (such as one from the pairs-transition list) to use with the transition procedures that follow.

Continue rotating between the regular three-day routine and the transition format until all Level C books are completed and then use the transition process with Level D books for the remainder of the school year.

Steps for Coaching Pairs of Students

The reason for working with only two children at a time is that the children get more practice with independent reading in groups of two than if they are in a group of six or seven. In a larger group, they would only get to read every sixth or seventh page as opposed to every other page when reading with only one other child. It would be wonderful if every child could read one-on-one with the teacher for transition reading. However, I have found that this takes more than three days, and you should still move on to a new story at the end of three days so the children feel challenged. Steps at this transition phase include:

1. Children take turns reading. Have each first grader read aloud the book "cold" and support each child's needs. Your role is to continue to help these pairs of students with the use of phonics and contextual analysis as needed.

2. After the children have each done the cold read with you, the coach you've trained takes over. He or she sits besides the student pairs and listens to the child read aloud, one at a time. The coach reinforces the children's efforts to sound out words and to use context to unlock meanings of unfamiliar words.

3. You move on to working with another pair if time permits.

4. Independent activities for all students, including the EIR children you are not working with as a pair, are provided in Chapter 7, and activities on the lesson planners for exemplar EIR books are in Appendix 4-6 on the DVD. Also, the children can reread old stories or read new ones independently or with a partner.

Tips for Teacher Coaching During the Transition Phase

Keep the following points in mind to guide your instruction in the transition phase:

▶ Ask questions that will help the child become self-reliant and successful in word attack.

▶ Don't jump in too quickly to try to "save" a child's disfluent reading aloud or if the student pauses. Teacher interruptions interfere with the flow of the reading. However, reading that is too far off-base becomes very confusing to the reader. Balance is the key (and the art) of effective coaching.

▶ Remind the child to reread from the beginning of a sentence after pausing to work on a word.

▶ Give children enough wait time. Often if you are patient, you will find that children are able to figure out unknown words, especially because of the emphasis in EIR on using strategies to attack words.

As you coach during the transition phase, try to use more general prompts first and move to more specific prompts only if needed. The reason for this is that you want to foster children's independence. You are not really helping them become independent if you suggest a specific strategy to try. A list of more general prompts for strategies is provided below.

As children are engaged in transition reading, there is a fair amount of variation in individuals' reading abilities. There is no need to be concerned. Just remind yourself that the children started at different places in the fall. What *is* important is that as many of your students in EIR as possible are reading independently by the end of the school year.

By way of example, Celia introduces a story about two cats with Nick and Chase. This is a book they have never read before. "We are going to find out who the cats are and what they like to do." Chase reads fairly well. He sounds out /gr/, /a/, /n/, /d/ in *grandma*. Celia has him go back when he gets to the end of the sentence. "Does that make sense? They where going to sleep at grandma and grandpa's house?" Chase corrects himself, "They were . . ." Celia coaches, "That is what good readers do, they go back and check if it doesn't make sense."

tips

You may want to make a Before and During Reading Prompts chart to hang in the classroom so all students can benefit.

tips

Praise for self-corrections, successful attempts, and unsuccessful attempts (point out a part that is right); success with coaching depends on you.

General Prompt to Use Before Reading—Transition Phase

▶ What can you do if it's getting really confusing or if a word doesn't seem right?

General Prompts to Use As Students Are Reading—Transition Phase

▶ What can you do that can help you? (Reread, keep reading and come back, think about what would make sense, sound out, etc.)

▶ Is there something you read on this page that isn't right? What can you do about it?

▶ Does the word you just read sound right and look right? Why or why not?

▶ Does that make sense? Think of the story. Think of what's happening.

▶ What can you do to make the word easier/shorter? Is there an ending you can cover up? Is there a word part you recognize? Can you break it into two words (if it's a compound word) or chunks?

When Chase pauses at *asked*, Celia tells him, "Cover up the ending." Chase is able to sound out *ask* and then reads *asked*.

Nick stumbles on a few words. When he reads *both* with a short *o*, Celia tells him to try another sound for *o*. He comes up with *both*. "Does that make sense?" "Yes." "Now go back and reread as good readers do." She tells him to try another sound for *i*, and he comes up with *rides*. When he pauses on another word, Celia gives him a general prompt to encourage him. "Keep going, you are doing very well."

After the boys have read the story, Celia coaches for comprehension by asking them to each tell about a part of the story they liked.

see it iN Action

video
16

Transition Phase: Independent Reading

Celia reads with two more boys who are stronger readers than those in the first example. Before the students take turns reading, she reviews the strategies that good readers use. They don't need much coaching, so Celia does not interrupt very much. However, when Andy reads, "Kit and Kat go out their stuff," she says, "You read, Kit and Kat go out their stuff. Does that make sense?" Andy quickly comes up with *got*. When Jake stumbles, Celia says, "Good readers make mistakes, so that is okay. But you need to go back and figure it out like good readers do." At the end, she coaches for comprehension by asking them what they like to do with a grandparent, uncle, or older person who is a friend.

The End Goal: Building Reading Stamina over the Summer

A major objective of the transition phase in first grade is to have children leave school for the summer feeling confident about their ability to read independently so they will continue to read over the summer. Often first graders in EIR are slow to realize they can actually pick up a book they have never seen before and read it. Sometimes they feel they can only read a book that has been read to them first. This is the notion you are trying to get them beyond as you focus on the transition phase of EIR. A summer reading list appears on the DVD (Appendix 5-1), which illustrates the types of books that will support EIR students' reading over the summer.

Additional Strategies for Word Recognition Instruction

Once students are developing independence as readers, you need to help them with vowel combinations. Also, you can conduct oral reading analysis to pinpoint decoding strengths and weaknesses of individual children that you can focus on as you coach them during transition reading

Introducing the Advanced Vowel Chart

After students have become fairly comfortable with using the short vowel chart (refer back to Chapter 3) and with decoding CVC words and CVCE words during the three-day repeated reading cycle for EIR lessons at EIR Levels A and B, you want to focus on one-syllable words that contain vowel pairs in your word work instruction and your word recognition coaching instruction with books at Levels C and D, especially during the transition phase. As you move to vowel pairs, you introduce the advanced vowel chart in which the most common sounds for vowel pairs are presented (see the next page). When students are trying to decode a word like *show*, have them use the advanced vowel chart to try one sound for *ow* (as in *cow*) and if that doesn't sound right try the other sound (as in *snow*).

Oral Reading Analysis and Instruction

Until students are reading in the transition phase, they usually are successful with EIR books because they have been reading them repeatedly. However, they typically are not yet reading independently, or on their own (e.g., decoding books that they have never read or heard before with at least 92 percent accuracy and that are at a Guided Reading Levels of D or higher). Once students can read at a primer level (e.g., decoding books they have not read before that are at Guided Reading Levels F G H), it is informative to conduct an oral reading analysis to take a look at what decoding strengths and weaknesses individual students have when they are reading independently (Taylor et al. 1995). This can be done during an oral reading check (see pages 90–93 in Chapter 6). In oral reading analysis, you take three, 100-word samples of a student's reading of material at their instructional level (92 percent–97 percent accuracy in word recognition) or at least above the frustration level over several days. (Reading below 90% accuracy is reading at a frustration level [Leslie and Caldwell 2006].) You analyze these samples to determine one problem area to focus on and then provide instruction in this focus area (see Figure 5-3). As a student does subsequent oral readings, you continue to assess in this focus area. Once a student has made good progress in one problem area, move to another as needed. The procedures for oral reading analysis follow and a chart you can use to take notes when you conduct oral reading analysis is in Figure 5-4.

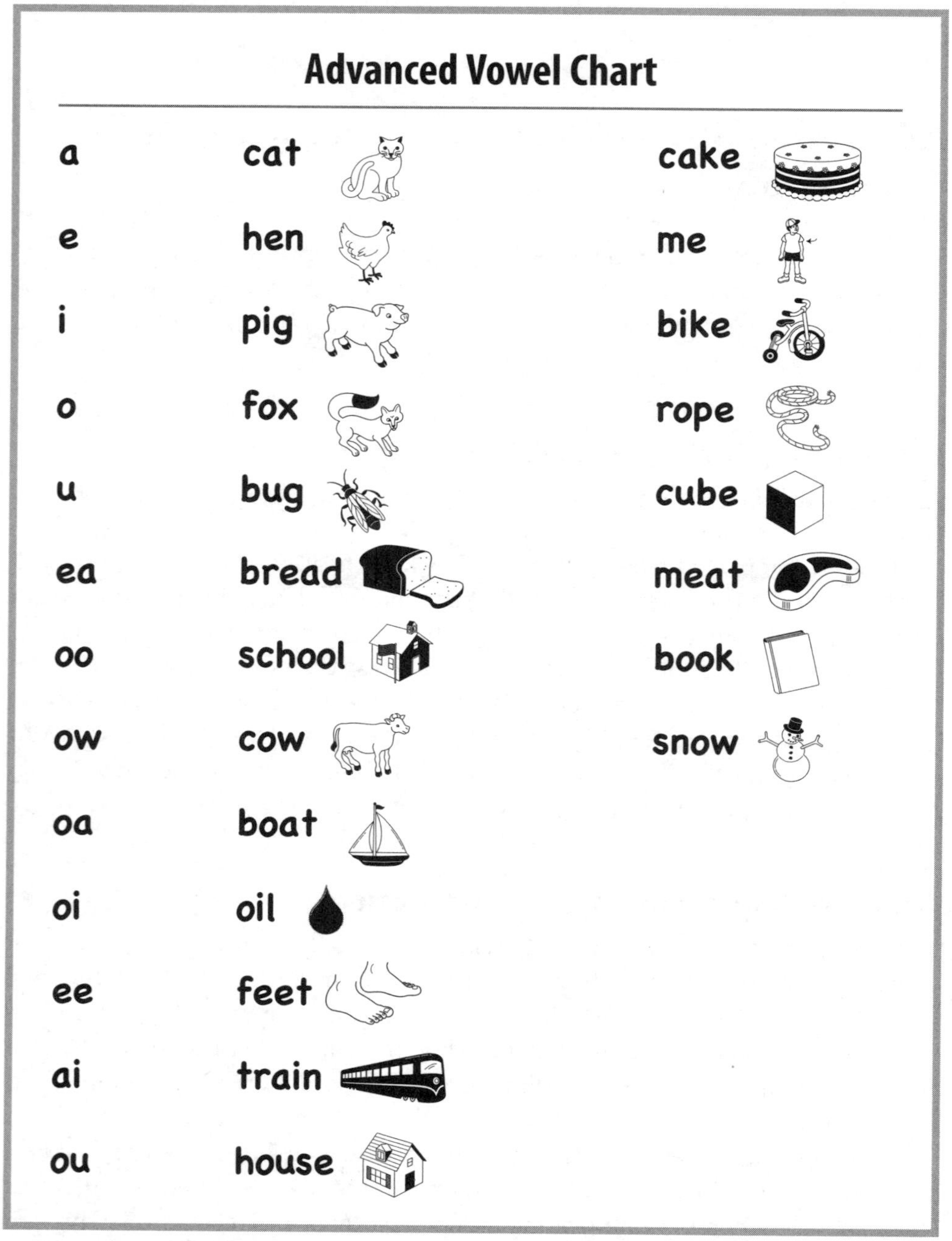

Advanced Vowel Chart

a	cat	cake
e	hen	me
i	pig	bike
o	fox	rope
u	bug	cube
ea	bread	meat
oo	school	book
ow	cow	snow
oa	boat	
oi	oil	
ee	feet	
ai	train	
ou	house	

Figure 5-2 Advanced Vowel Chart

Using Oral Reading Analysis to Target Your Teaching During the Transition Phase

If you have students who are still struggling with word recognition during the transition phase, as will be true for most students who are in you EIR group, conduct an oral reading analysis (Taylor et al. 1995). The steps are as follows:

▶ Take three, 100-word samples of a student's reading of material at their instructional level (92 percent to 97 percent accuracy in word recognition).

▶ Analyze these samples to determine one problem area to focus on.

▶ Provide instruction in this focus area.

▶ As a student does subsequent oral readings, continue to assess in this focus area, monitoring with a progress chart to document the student's growth in the target area.

▶ Once a student has made good progress in one problem area, move to another as needed. Potential problem areas and recommendations for instruction are included here.

Recording Errors for Oral Reading Analysis

The following is an example of a child's reading of a story. (What the child reads is in parentheses.) A self-correction (SC) is not counted as an error. Note that the child has read this story with 90 percent accuracy, so it is at the appropriate level for oral reading analysis (35 words correct/38 words = 92 percent word recognition accuracy). In the example that follows, a child's decoding errors are provided above the text. The chart showing the child's reading is then analyzed. A blank recording sheet that you can use to take notes when you conduct oral reading analysis can be found on the DVD.

Pup and Bud

(bad)   **(go) SC**
It is a big day for Pup. He is going to play at Bud's house.

(Pud) SC (pecks)   **(resting)**
Pup packs a bag of toys. Pup is ready to go.

His dad takes him to Bud's house. Pup and Bud have fun.

SC = child self-corrects

Oral Reading Analysis
Type of Error and Problem/Instruction and Ongoing Assessment

Type of Error and Problem	Instruction/Ongoing Assessment
Analysis. Student doesn't know how to look all the way through a word to analyze it.	This is the word recognition problem that is hardest to correct. Continue to model for a student how to analyze all the letters in a word. Continue to coach a student to look at the middle and end of a word, not just the beginning.
Automatic. Student makes many errors automatically; that is, the word comes out almost instantly, but it is the wrong word.	At the end of the page, ask the student if he knows what word he read very quickly but read incorrectly. If he does not, reread the sentence the way he read it as he reads along, and ask again. Typically, when a student sees what he is doing, he begins to read more carefully and makes fewer automatic errors.
Meaning. Student makes many errors that don't make sense.	At the end of a page, ask the student to identify which word in the sentence didn't make sense. Or, if needed, reread the sentence the way the child read it and ask if there is a word that doesn't make sense. Have him try to figure out the correct word, paying particular attention to the meaning of the text. Typically, once this problem is brought to the student's attention, the number of errors self-corrected goes up quite readily.
Basic sight word. Student makes many errors with basic sight words. (Often these are also automatic errors.)	Often a student doesn't believe he is doing this since he knows the words in isolation. Reread the sentence where the basic sight word was read incorrectly, and ask the child to tell you what word was incorrect. Talk about the problem of reading so quickly that errors are made.
Phonics: symbol-sound correspondence. Student makes consistent phonics errors in which he gives the wrong sound for a symbol.	Coach the student, with the use of the short or advanced vowel chart, as he corrects errors of this type.
Omission. Student skips over many or most hard words.	Often this is due to the fact that the student doesn't know how to attack longer words. Model and coach on how to decode a word completely, and praise a child when he does not skip over words.

© 2010 by Barbara M. Taylor from *Catching Readers, Grade 1*. Portsmouth, NH: Heinemann.

continues

Figure 5-3 *Oral Reading Analysis*

Oral Reading Analysis, *continued*
Completed Recording Chart

1 Error	2 Analysis Difficulty	3 Automatic Error	4 Meaning Error	5 Other Errors (basic sight words, phonic elements, omissions)	6 Notes
Big (bad)	X				The child quickly said the wrong word, thus it was an automatic error. He did not even take the time to analyze it. However, the error does make sense at this point in the story.
Going (go) SC					No error since the child self-corrected (SC).
Pud (Pup) SC					No error since the child self-corrected (SC).
Packs (pecks)		X		Child gave the short *e* sound instead of the short *a* sound.	The error does not make sense.
Ready (resting)	X				The child paused on the word, but he did not look through the word after the /r/ and /e/. He did not analyze the end of the work; hence this is an analysis difficulty.

Key to Columns in Chart

1. **Error.** Error due to the substitution of a real word or nonword for the actual word. Substitution is written above in parentheses. (*SC* is used to indicate a self-correction. *SD* is used to indicate a word the student had to stop on to decode, but the student was successful in coming up with the word without even making a self-correction.) If a word is omitted, draw a circle around it.

2. **Analysis Difficulty.** The student does not seem to be able to work through the entire word but is only able to decode part of it. Error is marked with X in column 2.

3. **Automatic Error.** The student quickly reads the word so that it comes out automatically. However, the word is not read correctly. Error is marked with an X in column 3.

4. **Meaning Error.** The student comes up with a real word or nonword that really doesn't make sense in the context of the text being read. Error is marked with an X in column 4. Be somewhat liberal here. For example, I would not count *bad* for *big* on the first page of the story as a meaning error since the reader had not read enough yet to know that it was not a bad day. However, this involves personal judgment and I realize that some would want to count it as a meaning error, especially if they had done a brief picture walk before reading the story. I just tell people to try to be consistent in how they score errors.

5. **Other Errors.** Typically, there are errors in which the students gave the wrong sound for the symbol (phonic element error) gave the wrong word for a basic sight word (basic sight word error) or omitted a word (omission).

6. **Notes.** Here is a place to make comments about the students' reading.

Figure 5-3 Oral Reading Analysis: Sample of a Completed Recording Chart, *continued*

Oral Reading Analysis Recording Sheet

1 Error	2 Analysis Difficulty	3 Automatic Error	4 Meaning Error	5 Other Errors (basic sight words, phonic elements, omissions)	6 Notes

Figure 5-4 Blank Oral Reading Analysis Recording Sheet

What Do We Learn? What's the Focus for Instruction?

It would be best to look across the student's three samples before making a decision about where to focus instruction. Also, this is a personal decision. There is no right answer about where to focus first. However, because in EIR "Does it make sense?" is always emphasized, I would not expect the student to say *pecks* for *packs* as show in Figure 5-3. After a child's progress chart had shown improvement in this area, I would perhaps focus and chart progress on the times the child gave the correct short vowel sound in less familiar words he had to decode.

Summary

The transition phase is an exciting and challenging time for young readers. While their reading skills are improving and their independence is growing, it is important to continue to support and scaffold their growth, since with this added independence students sometimes can become frustrated. The continued coaching, working with word-recognition strategies, and the conducting of an analysis of students oral reading will enable you to continue the needed support these budding readers need.

Now that you have an idea about the three-day routine and the transition phase, Chapter 6 addresses assessment procedures for selecting students for EIR, monitoring progress of students in EIR, and if enough progress is made, having students exit from EIR.

Assessing First Graders in EIR

• •

In this chapter, I share the fall assessments that help you determine which first graders will benefit from supplemental reading instruction, as well as advice for monitoring their reading progress during the year and in the spring.

Fall Assessments

In September, teachers assess first graders to see if there are students who would benefit from this supplemental instruction. These assessments are typical of the kinds of classroom-based assessments teachers give their students at the beginning of the school year. However, to be as certain as you can that the right students are getting supplemental reading help through EIR lessons, you should give these assessments to the children whom you think may need the added support to succeed in reading in first grade. Research has found that letter name knowledge and level of phonemic awareness are the best two predictors of end-of-first-grade reading achievement (Adams 1990; Snow, Burns, and Griffin 1998). For this reason, we use measures of these two abilities, along with

letter–sound knowledge and teacher judgment, to help decide which students would benefit from EIR.

All assessments are administered individually, and they are best given in the morning when children are less tired. Other children can be working on independent reading activities during this time. Starting with the easiest assessments, you first assess students' knowledge of letter names and sounds. This takes about five minutes (see Figure 6-1 here and a reproducible version on the DVD). Note that all figures in this chapter are also available as full-size reproducibles DVD for your teaching needs. Next, you would give the Classroom Phonemic Awareness Test, which takes about ten minutes (Figure 6-2). You do not have to do both assessments on the same day. The assessments are briefly described here, and explicit directions for administering them appears in Figure 6-3 on page 85.

The Letter Name and Letter Sound Assessment

This assessment is easy to administer and you will be able to move quickly through it with students. Starting with the column of uppercase letters, you ask a child to tell you the names of the letters. Then you move to the column of lowercase letters and ask the child to tell you the names of the lowercase letters. Finally, you go to the column labeled *consonant sounds* and ask the child to give you the sound each consonant makes.

Letter Name and Letter Sound Scoring Sheet

Letter Name—Upper*		Letter Name—Lower*		Consonant Sounds**	
K		k		k	
G		g		g	
A		a		g	
P		p		p	
W		w		w	
B		b		b	
H		h		h	
C		c		c	
I		i		c	
J		j		j	
Y		y		y	
L		l		l	
Q		q		qu	
M		m		m	
D		d		d	
N		n		n	
S		s		s	
X		x		x	
F		f		f	
Z		z		z	
R		r		r	
V		v		v	
T		t		t	
E		e		e	
O		o		o	
U		u		u	

Total Correct _____

*Check if known
**Check if known (ask for two different sounds for g and c)

Figure 6-1 *Letter Name and Letter Sound Scoring Sheet*

Classroom Phonemic Awareness Test

Name _____   Teacher _____

Blending Assessment

Example: When I say *c - a - b*, can you tell me the word?

1. t - a - p		Teacher says t - a - p
2. s - e - t		Teacher says s - e - t
3. f - i - b		Teacher says f - i - b
4. j - o - g		Teacher says j - o - g
5. c - u - t		Teacher says c - u - t
6. s - o - f - t		Teacher says s - o - f - t

Number correct _____

Segmentation Assessment

Example: When I say *sad*, can you give each sound you hear in the word?

7. p - a - t		Teacher says *pat*
8. b - e - t		Teacher says *bet*
9. s - i - p		Teacher says *sip*
10. p - o - d		Teacher says *pod*
11. t - u - b		Teacher says *tub*
12. f - a - s - t		Teacher says *fast*

Number correct _____

Figure 6-2 *Classroom Phonemic Awareness Test*

The Classroom Phonemic Awareness Test

I developed this test almost twenty years ago, and have found it to be especially useful in identifying children who are in need of supplemental reading instruction in first grade (see the DVD for a reproducible version of the assessment). The test takes about ten minutes to administer.

My research suggests that without a program like EIR, children who score 5 or less on this 12-item test in September of first grade are at considerable risk of failing to learn to read during the school year (Taylor 1991). In fact, the test predicts with about 85 percent accuracy that those who score 5 or lower on the test will have difficulty learning to read. This test also predicts with about 90 percent accuracy that those who score 8 or higher on the test will be reading well by the end of the year. Additional information on how to administer this test along with information on its reliability and validity are provided on the DVD; see Research: A Test of Phonemic Awareness for Classroom Use (Taylor 1991).

See Figure 6-3 for directions for the fall assessments (a full-size reproducible version can be found on the DVD). A blank summary sheet can be found in Figure 6-4 and on the DVD.

Administration Directions for EIR Fall Assessments

Step 1. **Administer the letter name portion of the assessment** (see Figure 6-1).

  a. Begin with the uppercase letters. Say to the child, "I'd like you to tell me the names of these letters. What letter is this?" (Note: You may point to the letter.)

  b. Do not provide any help or tell the child if the answer is right or wrong.

  c. Record the *correct response* with a check mark. If the child gives the incorrect letter, record the letter the child gave. If the child cannot or will not give a response, record 0.

  d. Discontinue testing if a child is unable to identify ten *consecutive* letters.

  e. Repeat the process with the lowercase letters.

  f. Record the total number correct for upper- and lowercase letters.

Step 2. **Administer the letter sound portion of the assessment** (see Figure 6-1).

  a. Say to the child, "I'd like you to tell me the sounds of these letters. What sound does this letter make?" (Note: You may point to the letter.). For *g* and *c* you ask for the two common sounds each letter makes.

  b. Do not provide any help or tell the child if the answer is right or wrong.

  c. Record the correct response with a check mark. If the child gives the incorrect sound, record the sound the child gave. If the child cannot or will not give a response, record 0.

  d. Discontinue testing if a child is unable to identify ten *consecutive* sounds.

  e. Record the number of correctly identified letter sounds.

Step 3. **Administer the blending section of the Classroom Phonemic Awareness Test** (Taylor 1991). (See Figure 6-2).

  a. Do the example as follows: Begin by saying to the child, "I am going to give you some sounds and I would like you to put the sounds together into a word. For example, when I say /c/ /a/ /b/, can you tell me the word?" If the child is unable to respond or responds incorrectly, the teacher does the practice item for the child. "The sounds /c/ /a/ /b/ would go together to make the word *cab*. Now you try the next one."

  b. Have the child do items 1–6.

  • After each item, write the child's response.

  • If the response is incorrect or the child is unable to do the item, the teacher does *not* correct the child or do the task correctly for the child. However, you could return to the practice item.

  • An item must be totally correct to be scored as correct. If, for example, in number two, if the child says *sat* for *set*, it is not counted as correct.

  c. Record the number correct.

continues

Figure 6-3 Administration Directions for EIR Fall Assessments

See the DVD for full-size versions of all the forms in this chapter.

BEFORE YOU BEGIN

Tips for Administering the Classroom Phonemic Awareness Test

▶ *Pronounce each word naturally.* When giving the blending portion of the Classroom Phonemic Awareness Test, you should pronounce each sound but exaggerate the sounds as little as possible.

▶ *Practice with a colleague.* Teachers have found that it works well to practice giving the test to one another before they administer it to children.

▶ *Practice on a proficient first grader.* Teachers have told me that practicing with an average student who they know will do well on the test helps build their confidence that they are administering the test soundly. That is, when they test a less-skilled child who ends up doing poorly on the test, they are less likely to think the weak performance was due to them.

▶ *Start the blending portion of the test by saying something along these lines:* "When I say c - a - b, can you tell me the word?" If a child can't tell you, do it for her. You can return to the practice item to review with the child what he is supposed to do, but don't provide the answers for missed items on the test itself. Here is how I would say the other items on the blending subtest: t - a - p, s - e - t, f - i - b, j - o - g, c - u - t, s - o - f - t. Again, pronounce each sound but exaggerate the sounds as little as possible.

▶ *Start the segmentation portion of the test by saying something like this:* "When I say *sad* can you give each sound you hear in the word? What sound do you hear first in *sad?* What sound do you hear next in *sad?* What sound do you hear at the end of *sad?*" If a child can't do this, do it for him. If you need to you can return to the practice item to review what the child is to do. Also, if you need to, you can continue to say throughout the test, "What do you hear first in *pat?* What do you hear next in *pat?* What do you hear at the end of *pat?*" If a child gives you the letter name, tell him this is correct, but ask him to give you the sound this letter makes. Demonstrate again that the first sound in *sad* is /s/, the second sound is /a/, and the end sound is /d/.

Fall Summary Sheet

Student	Phoneme Blending Score (PB)	Phoneme Segmentation Score (PS)	PB + PS Score	Letter Name Score	Letter Sound Score	In EIR (check)

Figure 6-4 Fall Summary Sheet

Looking at Scores to See Which Children May Need EIR

Now I want to share recommendations to help you identify students who would benefit from EIR lessons based on years of research on EIR. Also, if you are not sure, I recommend you put a child in an EIR group as opposed to keeping him out of one. It is better to have a child quit coming to EIR lessons because he is reading so well than to have him get way behind in reading because he has not been in an EIR group.

How Do I Use the Results of the Classroom Phonemic Awareness Test?

Students with a score of 5 or less. I have found that first graders who score 5 or less on this test are in need of an effective reading intervention.

Students who score 0, 1, or 2. These students need the intervention the most. In high-poverty schools, teachers have often reported to me that 50 percent to 75 percent of their students score 5 or lower on the test, so don't be alarmed if this is what you find in your classroom.

Students who score 6 or 7. If you have room in your EIR group, children who score 6 or 7 on the Classroom Phonemic Awareness Test should be included. These may be children who will quit coming to EIR lessons before the end of the school year. Please see page 94 for more guidelines for students who need EIR for shorter stretches of the year.

A word of caution: I must caution you that the cutoff scores of 5 or below and 8 or above on the Classroom Phonemic Awareness Test are based on the premise that the assessment is done in the first month of first grade and that it is administered according to the procedures outlined in this chapter. If you administer the test more leniently (e.g., provide correct responses to missed items as you go through the test), I cannot tell you how to interpret the scores. Also, I do not know how well the cutoff scores of 5 and 8, based on a test administration at the end of kindergarten, predict end-of-first-grade reading achievement. I do know, however, that many children will grow in phonemic awareness from the end of kindergarten to the beginning of first grade.

How Do I Use the Results of the Letter Name and Letter–Sound Recognition Assessment?

I have found the letter name test less useful (but still a proxy for a child's literacy environment prior to school) because so many children are drilled on letter names in preschool and kindergarten. If a child knows almost all of his letter names but gets a very low score on the phonemic awareness test, he will likely have trouble learning to read.

I have found the letter–sound test, which focuses on the consonants, to provide me with more helpful information for identifying children for EIR than the letter name portion of the test. Over the years, children receiving grade 1 EIR lessons have identified 8 letter sounds, on average in the fall. So, for example, if I have two children who scored 5 on the phonemic awareness test and only one opening in my EIR group, I'd put the child who knew only 5 letter sounds as opposed the one who knew 10, in EIR.

Assessing Students' Progress in Reading During the School Year

It is always important to continually assess students' progress; therefore, embedded within the EIR model are opportunities for teachers to monitor and document students' progress. Oral reading checks for word recognition accuracy, oral reading analysis, and oral reading fluency checks are three assessments recommended when implementing EIR. Oral reading analysis is discussed in Chapter 5. Oral reading checks and oral reading fluency assessments are discussed in this chapter.

It is important to note that the oral reading analysis and oral reading fluency are not really useful until a child is reading independently at the transition to independent reading phase discussed in Chapter 5. Until students are reading independently (e.g., reading books "cold" at the transition phase), they are successful with their EIR stories, in part, because they have read them repeatedly. You cannot get an accurate indication of their word recognition strengths or weaknesses or their reading rate when they have read a story multiple times over three days.

The following are some grouping considerations covered in Chapter 3 that are worth revisiting:

✓ *Keep the groups no bigger than seven students.* Orchestrate two groups, if need be. Perhaps the Title 1 teacher can take one group and you can take the other. Then you can periodically switch groups so you have a sense of the strengths and weaknesses of all your struggling readers.

✓ *Reserve EIR instruction for teachers only.* Children at risk of reading failure desperately need quality, supplemental reading instruction from a certified teacher. Instructional aides don't have sufficient background.

✓ *Arrange two groups for optimum student participation.* If you have enough students for two groups, put the faster-progressing students in one group and the students who may need more support in the other. In this way, it won't always be the more advanced students calling out answers at the expense of the slower-progressing students. Also, the slower-progressing students are less inclined to feel discouraged if they do not experience others in their group catching on more quickly.

✓ *Remember, children who become on-grade-level readers can be taken out of the EIR group.* Some students will catch up to their grade-level peers and therefore not need EIR beyond, say, February, sometimes even sooner. Guidelines to help you decide if children are ready to be taken out of EIR are provided later in this chapter on page 94.

✓ *ELL students do well in EIR (Taylor 2001).* Often the question comes up as to what to do with ELLs and fall placement in EIR. It is true that ELLs, especially children such as Hmong students whose first language sounds are very different from English, will score more poorly on the phonemic awareness assessment than would be the case if they were native English speakers. On the other hand, even if ELLs do relatively poorly on the fall assessment, I would put them in an EIR group in the fall unless they have the opportunity to learn to read in their first language. If possible, I might use something like the kindergarten EIR program (Taylor forthcoming, also see Lessons for Students Who Need Additional Phonemic Awareness Instruction in Appendix 3-1 on the DVD) to develop oral vocabulary and emergent literacy skills at the same time, but not instead of, their participation in grade 1 EIR lessons. You do not want to take the chance of preventing any student from learning to read by postponing their participation in EIR to a later time, such as after the first of the year.

✓ *Special education students do well in EIR.* I have also found EIR works well with students who have learning disabilities. No modifications to the program are recommended. However, students who are developmentally and cognitively delayed learn well in EIR, but more predictable texts are typically needed than those used in regular EIR lessons to keep the children feeling successful. I would start out with the regular books at EIR Level A and switch to more predictable books, if needed, as the regular EIR stories at Levels B and C are more challenging.

✓ *The earlier the better.* Sometimes teachers ask me if they should wait to put a child in EIR since he or she scored so low on all the assessments. My response is always, "No, put them in EIR in the fall." If you wait to put your lowest students in EIR in January, for example, you are likely ensuring that they will not catch on to reading in first grade. I, for one, do not want to make that decision for any child. I want to give them all a chance to learn to read in first grade.

Conducting Oral Reading Checks

Regular monitoring of progress is an important part of EIR. We use oral reading checks with the children in EIR to see who is making good progress in the program. *An oral reading check should be taken on every child about every other story on average during Step 1 of Days, 1, 2, and/or 3 of the EIR routine.* The oral reading check should be taken on the story just finished and within a few days after moving on to a new story.

In EIR, the oral reading check is first and foremost to monitor children's progress rather than to do an analysis of errors. In first grade, children reading "old" EIR stories with at least 90 percent accuracy are making good progress.

At first, children in first grade may not do as well as hoped for on their oral reading check, but after a few, you should see them moving above the 90 percent accuracy mark. If a child is consistently falling below 90 percent accuracy on his oral reading check, he is a child who needs more individual help. Perhaps this is a child you attend to more often during the time you coach individuals. Perhaps this is a child who works more than once a day with a one-on-one coach. This is also a child who would benefit from one-on-one tutoring if that is available at your school.

To take an oral reading check, you can simply make check marks on a sheet of paper for words read correctly. For words read incorrectly, write the word the child actually says. If a child self-corrects, mark this with "SC" next to the word read incorrectly that you wrote down. If you end up telling a child a word, mark this with a "TH" for teacher help.

During an oral reading check, tell the child that you won't be coaching as much as you usually do because you want to see what the child can do on her own. If a child is getting very mixed up, you can coach (or tell a child a word if it is a hard word), but try to do this sparingly for the oral reading check. If a child is very frustrated, you can stop. However, you should try to get the child to read through the story if possible.

Count errors, including words you did have to tell the child, but do not include repetitions or self-corrections in this count. Out of the total number of words read, subtract the number of errors to determine the total number of words read correctly. Divide the number of words read correctly out of the number of words read to get the word recognition accuracy score.

In first grade, a child is at the frustration level when she falls below 90 percent accuracy in word recognition (Leslie and Caldwell 2006). Often I find that children who are struggling in reading are given books to read that are at their frustration level. An Oral Reading Check summary sheet is provided in Figure 6-5 and can also be found, along with the previous procedures, on the DVD as a reproducible form.

An Example of an Oral Reading Check

What follows is an oral reading check for the sample reading beneath the check marks. The *TH* is used to indicate that the child was told the word *stuff* by the teacher (teacher help). The *SC* is used to indicate that the child first read *go* for *going* but then self-corrected.

✓ ✓ ✓ bad ✓ ✓ ✓

✓ ✓ go (SC) ✓ ✓ ✓ ✓ ✓

Pud (SC) pecks ✓ ✓ ✓ ✓

✓ ✓ resting ✓ ✓

✓ ✓ ✓ ✓ ✓ ✓ ✓

✓ ✓ ✓ ✓ ✓

35 words correct/38 words = 92 percent word recognition accuracy

Pup and Bud

    (bad)
It is a big day for Pup.

    (go) SC
He is going to play at Bud's house.

(Pud) SC (pecks)
Pup packs a bag of toys.

    (resting)
Pup is ready to go.

His dad takes him to Bud's house.

Pup and Bud have fun.

Oral Reading Check Summary Sheet

Student	Level		Level		Level		Level	
	Story		Story		Story		Story	
	% Word Recognition Accuracy Score	Date Given	% Word Recognition Accuracy Score	Date Given	% Word Recognition Accuracy Score	Date Given	% Word Recognition Accuracy Score	Date Given

Figure 6-5 Oral Reading Check Summary Sheet

Assessing Word Recognition Fluency

Skilled readers are fluent readers. They are able to read orally with accuracy, automaticity, speed, proper phrasing, and expression. *Automaticity* means the reader recognizes a word automatically while reading. The benefit of fluent reading is that it enables a reader to devote maximum cognitive capacity to the meaning of text (Kuhn and Stahl 2003; NRP 2000). Less-fluent readers focus attention on decoding individual words and tend to read in a choppy, word-by-word manner.

One good measure of fluent reading is the number of words read correctly on a grade-level passage in one minute (wcpm score). The number of words read correctly in a minute has been found to be a useful indicator of a student's reading ability (Fuchs et al. 2001). Once a student is in the transition phase in EIR lessons, you can measure his reading rate in terms of wcpm scores when you have him read passages "sight unseen" from grade-level texts or other materials designed to assess fluency. Also, as part of the EIR spring assessments, you will get measures of a student's oral reading rate in the form of wcpm scores, when you have them read passages from an informal reading inventory. By the end of the school year, you want to see students reading at about 50 words correct per minute or better.

Mean Word Correct per Minute Scores and Standard Deviations (in parenthesis)

Grade	Mean Fall Score	Mean Winter Score	Mean Spring Score
1		23 (32)	53 (39)
2	51 (37)	72 (41)	89 (42)
3	71 (40)	92 (43)	107 (44)
4	94 (40)	112 (41)	123 (43)
5	110 (45)	127 (44)	139 (45)

Adapted from Table 1 from Hasbrouck, J., and G. A. Tindal. 2006. "Oral Reading Fluency Norms: A Valuable Assessment Tool for Reading Teachers." *The Reading Teacher* 59 (7): 636–44.

Table 6-1 Mean Word Correct per Minute Scores and Standard Deviations

Hasbrouck and Tindal (2006) published fall, winter, and spring oral reading norms expressed in words correct per minute for more than 15,000 students in grades 1 through 5. The mean scores and standard deviations (in parentheses) are presented here in Table 6-1.

In addition to assessing students' reading fluency through a words correct per minute score, you can also use a rubric to assess student phrasing and expression while reading. The rubric developed by the National Assessment of Educational Practice (NAEP) follows in Figure 6-6.

NAEP's Oral Reading Fluency Scale

Level 4 Reads primarily in larger, meaningful phrase groups. Although some regressions, repetitions, and deviations from text may be present, these do not appear to detract from the overall structure of the story. Preservation of the author's syntax is consistent. Some or most of the story is read with expressive interpretation.

Level 3 Reads primarily in three- or four-word phrase groups. Some smaller groupings may be present. However, the majority of phrasing seems appropriate and preserves the syntax of the author. Little or no expressive interpretation is present.

Level 2 Reads primarily in two-word phrases with some three- or four-word groupings. Some word-by-word reading may be present. Word groupings may seem awkward and unrelated to larger context of sentence or passage.

Level 1 Reads primarily word by word. Occasional two-word or three-word phrases may occur, but these are infrequent and/or they do not preserve meaningful syntax.

Figure 6-6 NAEP's Oral Reading Fluency Scale

Taking a Child out of EIR

Often people ask how to decide if a child should quit going to EIR lessons because she is reading so well. The following guidelines will help you make this decision. There will be some children who no longer need EIR by January or February, but I have not found this to be too common. In general, however, I recommend that you be conservative and not take a child out of EIR too quickly.

Criteria for Taking a Child out of EIR

You may decide it is time for a child to stop coming to EIR lessons because she is reading very well and the EIR lessons seem too easy. Criteria to consider include the following:

▶ The child is able to read the "new" book or books of the week with 99 percent to 100 percent accuracy at least three weeks in a row on an oral reading check.

▶ The child has had EIR lessons for at least three months.

▶ When working in a group, the child is clearly ahead of other children.

▶ The child's performance in the classroom reading program shows that he or she is performing effectively in grade-level texts. The child would have to be able to read grade-level texts with at least 92 percent to 100 percent accuracy. (To assess, do an oral reading check on the next story the child will be reading from the school's reading series. This story should be read "cold"; that is, the child has not read or had an adult read it to him or her.)

▶ The child is reading close to 50 words correct per minute.

▶ Watch closely to see if children you have released are making good progress in the regular program. If not, they may need to rejoin the EIR group.

Spring Assessments

In the spring you need to administer an informal reading inventory (e.g., QRI-4, Leslie and Caldwell 2006) to evaluate a student's reading (decoding) level, reading rate (fluency), and comprehension ability. Directions for spring assessments in grade 1 follow in Figure 6-7. A summary sheet to record scores is in Figure 6-8 and a summarizing scoring rubric to assess comprehension beyond a students' ability to answer questions is in Figure 6-9. These forms can also be found as reproducibles on the DVD.

If the student reads a primer passage with 90 percent word recognition accuracy or greater, continue to an end-of-grade 1 passage from an informal reading inventory and repeat Steps 1–6. Stop if the child falls below 90 percent accuracy in word recognition and do not do the summarizing or comprehension questions (continue to Steps 5 and 6).

Directions for Spring Assessment

Oral reading: Errors include substitutions, omissions, teacher-assisted or teacher-pronounced words. Self-corrections, repetitions, or hesitations are *not* errors.

Step 1. Have the student read a primer passage from an informal inventory for 1 minute. Put a check above each word read incorrectly (error). If a student is stuck on a word in this one-minute timing give about 5 seconds, then tell the word. Mark the last word read in the minute.

Step 2. Continue reading the passage to the end, marking the errors made. Now that you are no longer timing the student, use your own judgment on time before telling a word, but probably give about a 5-second time wait. Stop if the child falls below 90 percent word recognition accuracy on the primer passage and do not do the summarizing or comprehension questions (continue to Steps 5 and 6).

Step 3. Have the student summarize the story. Use a 4-point rubric to score (see summarizing sheet for rubric, Figure 6-9). Record score 1, 2, 3, or 4 on summary sheet for the rubric description that best fits the summary.

Step 4. Ask the student questions for the passage. Record the percent of questions correct on the summary sheet.

Step 5. Go back and count the number of words read correctly in one minute. Record on summary sheet.

Step 6. Go back and count the number of errors in total passage. Calculate word recognition accuracy. Record on summary sheet.

Step 7. If the student reads the primer passage with 90 percent word-recognition accuracy or better, continue to an end-of-grade 1 passage and repeat steps 1–6.

Figure 6-7 Directions for Spring Assessment

Grade 1 Spring Assessment Summary Sheet

Grade 1	Primer Passage from an Informal Reading Inventory				End-of-Grade 1 Passage from an Informal Reading Inventory			
Student	Words Correct in First Minute	Word Recognition Accuracy (% Correct)	Summarizing Score Based on 4-Point Rubric	Questions Correct (%)	Words Correct in First Minute	Word Recognition Accuracy (% Correct)	Summarizing Score Based on 4-Point Rubric	Questions Correct (%)

Figure 6-8 Grade 1 Spring Assessment Summary Sheet

Summarizing Rubric for Grades 1–4

Passage _____ Child _____

Summarizing: Say, "Summarize the most important ideas you just read about."

Record student's response as best as possible:

Score:

1	2	3	4
✓ Student offers little or no information about the selection. ✓ Summary is incomprehensible. ✓ Stated ideas do not relate to the selection.	✓ Student relates details only. ✓ Student is unable to recall the gist of the selection. ✓ Summary is incomplete or ideas are misconstrued.	✓ Student relates some main ideas and some supporting details. ✓ Summary is fairly coherent.	✓ All major points and appropriate supporting details are included. ✓ High degree of completeness and coherence. ✓ Student generalizes beyond the text.

Figure 6-9 Summarizing Rubric for Grades 1–4

Guidelines for Monitoring Students' Progress in Spring

When considering students' reading progress, you first are looking for children's ability to decode a primer (e.g., Guided Reading Level G–H) or first-grade level (e.g., Guided Reading Level H–I) passage with at least 90 percent accuracy (see page 64 for the book levels chart). Our hope is that EIR grade 1 children, including ELL students and students with learning disabilities, are reading at a primer reading level or better by the end of the year. Over the years, I have found that on average 72 percent of the children in the grade 1 EIR intervention are reading on at least a primer level by May. Out of the children I have followed into second grade, I have found that 94 percent are able to read second-grade material (Taylor 2001).

Second, you are looking at a child's fluency as measured by words correct per minute (wcpm). In a national study, Taylor et al. (2000) found that the average first grader on an informal reading inventory was able to read the end-of-grade 1 passage in May with 54 words correct per minute. In the Hasbrouck and Tindal (2006) report, they found that the average student read at 53 wcpm in spring of first grade.

Third, you are concerned about a child's comprehension as measured by answering passage questions and summarizing the passage. I would like to see a child answer at least 70 percent of the questions correctly from an informal reading inventory passage and get a summarizing score of 3 or 4. However, in the national study, we found that the average first-grade reader had a summarizing score of 2.5 (Taylor et al. 2000).

If a child is able to read primer-level passages with 90 percent accuracy or better, the child will likely be decoding second-grade material in the fall. If a child can decode a primer or grade 1–level passage with at least 90 percent accuracy in word recognition but has difficulty with comprehension and fluency, the child may benefit from an intervention in the fall of second grade such as Accelerated Grade 2 EIR lessons (see Taylor 2010a).

If a child is unable to read primer-level passages with 90 percent accuracy, the child will probably need to be in an intervention such as Basic Grade 2 EIR lessons and will probably need supplemental help in word recognition, fluency, and comprehension (see Taylor 2010a).

Summary

This chapter introduced you to the assessment procedures used to support and successfully implement EIR. Watching students closely as they tackle the complex task of learning to read is imperative so that your teaching can be informed by what students know and are able to do, as well as that which they are struggling. The multiple chances to assess students reading and comprehension throughout the EIR three-day cycle and transition phase provides a framework that offers your struggling readers with the best possible chances for success.

In the next chapter, we take a broader look at the teaching of reading so you will be able to dovetail what you learned at EIR with your regular reading instruction. Chapter 7 describes how EIR fits into a reading block.

Managing Your Reading Block with EIR

In this chapter, we look at how the EIR lessons fit within the reading block, reading/writing block, or literacy block. Teachers arrange their literacy time in ways that suit their individual teaching styles and students' needs, and the EIR lessons are effective in many different iterations of effective instruction. However, as discussed briefly in Chapter 1, some components are in place no matter what: whole-group instruction, small-group instruction (including guided reading and EIR lessons), and independent reading/work for students while the teacher is with small groups.

Take a look at your reading block schedule. Research shows that effective teachers *balance* whole-class and small-group instruction (Pressley et al. 2003; Taylor et al. 2007). My research also shows that too much time on whole-group instruction (e.g., 60 percent of the time or more) or too much time on small-group instruction (e.g., 85 percent of the time or more) is negatively related to students' reading growth (Taylor et al. 2000, 2007).

With this balance in mind, it's often most powerful to begin the reading block with a whole-group lesson in which you provided explicit instruction in a reading skill or strategy, using a high-quality trade book or literature from a basal

reader anthology. That is, you teach the reading skill or strategy in the context of engaging with and enjoying a story or piece of nonfiction. Then you can move into small guided reading groups to differentiate instruction, including follow-up instruction on the skill or strategy covered in the whole-group lesson (Taylor 2010c). You and in turn your students should be aware of the connection between whole-group, small-group, and one-on-one instruction; it should not be a hidden thread but a visible thread. Students are in a much better position to learn when you explicitly name the connection for them. For example, in a small guided reading group, Heather Peterson reads *The Crow and the Pitcher* to her whole class and they discuss the author's intended message. On their own, students work with a partner as they read a story at their reading level and focus again on the story's main message. Heather makes the explicit connection to the whole-group lesson by saying, "I am going to give you a story of your own to work on with a partner during independent work time. Read it carefully and think about what the author wants you to know. Include the character and setting in the beginning, the story problem in the middle, and the solution and author's message at the end." Later, in her above-average guided reading group, Heather explains, "Since we are talking about the author's big ideas, we are going to read more stories called *fables*. Fables have a message, or moral, the author wants you to know." Students read another fable, *The Moon and the Well*, and discuss the moral to this story with support from their teacher. Stating the purpose of the lesson at the outset in this manner is a powerful technique that is often overlooked by teachers.

✓ tips

Helpful Resources

Fountas, I. C., and G. S. Pinnell. 1996. *Guided Reading: Good First Teaching for All Children.* Portsmouth, NH: Heinemann.

Lapp, D., D. Fisher, and T. D. Wolsey. 2009. *Literacy Growth for Every Child: Differentiated Small-Group Instruction, K–6.* New York: Guilford.

Manning, M., G. Morrison, and D. Camp. 2009. *Creating the Best Literacy Block Ever.* New York: Scholastic.

Pressley, M. 2006. *Reading Instruction That Works: The Case for Balanced Teaching.* 3d ed. New York: Guilford.

Routman, R. 2008. *Teaching Essentials.* Portsmouth, NH: Heinemann.

———. 2003. *Reading Essentials.* Portsmouth, NH: Heinemann.

Serravallo, J. 2010. *Reading Instruction in Small Groups.* Portsmouth, NH: Heinemann.

Southall, M. 2009. *Differentiated Small-Group Reading Lessons.* New York: Scholastic.

Taberski, S. 2000. *On Solid Ground: Strategies for Teaching Reading K–3.* Portsmouth, NH: Heinemann.

Tyner, B. 2009. *Small-Group Reading Instruction: A Differentiated Teaching Model for Beginning and Struggling Readers.* Newark, DE: International Reading Association.

Tyner, B., and S. E. Green. 2005. *Small-Group Reading Instruction: A Differentiated Teaching Model for Intermediate Grade Reader, Grades 3–8.* Newark, DE: International Reading Association.

Walpole, S., and M. C. McKenna. 2009. *How to Plan Differentiated Reading Instruction: Resources for Grades K–3.* New York: Guilford.

Effective teachers use good classroom management practices (Pressley et al. 2003). There are many excellent professional books, such as those listed in the Tip box, that can help you develop and manage a dynamic literacy block, but for now, here are a few key components:

▶ Work with students to establish classroom rules and routines to minimize disruptions and to provide for smooth transitions within and between lessons.

▶ Use positive language and a motivating, engaging environment to impact students' behavior.

▶ Make a conscious effort to develop self-regulated, independent learners.

▶ Create a positive classroom atmosphere by demonstrating enthusiasm for learning, and have high expectations for your students.

MANAGEMENT IDEAS

Some of the primary-grade teachers I have worked with have engaged in the following practices to promote a constructive, classroom environment. Notice that teachers negotiate the criteria for behavior with students and refine it through the year. Some teachers generate and revise lists of expected behaviors and routines as a shared writing activity.

▶ Generate rules as a class during the first week of school.

▶ Read through classroom rules with students and talk about them at the morning meeting.

▶ Ask students to evaluate their actions after a discussion or activity, focusing on strengths and areas in need of improvement.

▶ Teach students how to compliment each other and encourage them to be respectful of one another.

▶ Have a brief class meeting at the end of the day and ask students how they thought their behaviors were that day, based on the rules they had generated as a class.

▶ Use routines and procedures to handle disruptions effectively and efficiently.

▶ Use routines and procedures to provide for smooth transitions within and between lessons.

▶ Show students that you care about them as individuals, but also let them know that you will be firm, holding them to high standards as learners and good citizens.

▶ Give specific, constructive feedback to students regularly, provide encouragement, and challenge them to think more deeply.

▶ Offer sincere praise to students, as a group or one-on-one, when they have demonstrated behaviors reflected in your classroom rules as well as in school goals defining the school community, often displayed when you enter a building.

Reading Block Schedules: Examples of Effective Balance

The three teachers you met in Chapter 2 typically start their reading block with a 20- to 30-minute whole-group lesson (often broken up with brief partner work) and then move into a few 20- to 30-minute small-group lessons in which they provide differentiated instruction that varies depending on students' reading abilities and needs. All three teachers also provide EIR lessons to their lowest readers. The three teachers explicitly state their lesson purposes in both whole- and small-group lessons. They move at an efficient pace, guided by lesson goals, and meet with all of their small groups every day. Each of the teacher's schedules is presented and a brief discussion details how the reading block might unfold.

Heather's Daily Reading Block Schedule

9:00–9:25	Whole-group lesson
9:25–9:45	Small-group 1
9:45–10:05	Small-group 2
10:05–10:25	Small-group 3
10:25–10:45	EIR lesson
10:50–11:00	Whole-class follow-up to whole-class lesson

Heather has a 120-minute reading block. She spends about 25 minutes a day on a whole-group lesson with a 5-minute sharing on follow-up activities related to this lesson at the end of the literacy block. She spends about 60 minutes a day on three guided reading groups and 20 minutes on one EIR group (which is a second shot of quality instruction for her struggling readers).

Average and above-average readers spend about 60 minutes a day on four independent learning activities that include independent reading and below-average readers spend about 40 minutes a day on the independent learning activities that also include independent reading. Sometimes they have follow-up work to complete related to their EIR lesson as one of their three independent activities.

Heather has a parent or senior citizen volunteer in her classroom during her reading block who listens to EIR students reread their EIR stories and provides assistance as students are engaged in independent work activities.

Heather's Typical Daily Reading Block at a Glance

Whole-Group Lesson (25 minutes + 5 minute follow-up at end of block)	Small-Group Lesson (20 minutes for each group using leveled texts)	EIR Lesson (20 minutes)	Group	Activities for Independent Work Time
Read basal reader selection, target comprehension strategy, teach vocabulary at point ofcontact, discuss high-level questions, review activities for work time	Teach phonics as needed, read text and coach in word recognition strategies, discuss vocabulary at point of contact, provide follow-up to comprehension strategy taught in whole group, discuss high-level questions about leveled text			
X	X		Above-average * readers	Activity 1: Reading or rereading, writing, discussing as follow-up to whole-group text
				Activity 2: Reading or rereading, writing, discussing as follow-up to small-group text
				Activity 3: Reading or rereading, writing, discussing text unrelated to whole- or small-group lesson
				Activity 4: Reading for pleasure from book of choice
X	X		Average readers*	Activity 1
				Activity 2
				Activity 3
				Activity 4
X	X		Below-average readers**	Activity 1
		X		Activity 2 or 3
				Activity 4

*10–20 minutes for each activity for a total of 60 minutes

**10–20 minutes for each activity for a total of 40 minutes

John's Daily Reading Block Schedule

9:00–9:35   Whole-group lesson
9:35–9:55   Small-group 1
9:55–10:15   Small-group 2
10:15–10:30   Small-group 3
10:30–10:50   EIR

John has a 110-minute reading block. He begins with a whole-group lesson that lasts for about 35 minutes. He then spends about 55 minutes on three guided reading groups and 20 minutes on one EIR group (which is a second shot of quality instruction for his struggling readers).

Linda's Daily Reading Block Schedule

9:00–9:30   Whole-group lesson
9:30–9:50   Small-group 1
9:50–10:15   Small-group 2
10:15–10:40   Small-group 3
12:10–12:30   EIR lesson

Linda spends 120 minutes on reading a day. She spends about 30 minutes a day on a whole-group lesson in the morning. She spends about 70 minutes with three guided reading groups. Linda has an educational assistant in her room in the morning to work with students who are at their seats. An ELL teacher also comes in for 30 minutes to work with two groups of students. After lunch, Linda works with one EIR group for 20 minutes and Title 1 teacher takes another EIR group to a small nearby classroom at this time. (Other students engage in independent reading and complete activities from morning literacy block at this time.)

Independent Activities

The amount of independent work time required, so teachers can spend quality time with small groups, warrants that the independent activities students are engaged in are challenging and motivating. Also, a common question that teachers ask as they embark upon EIR lessons for their struggling readers is, *What are my other students doing when I teach my EIR group?* Heather, John, and Linda all reported that a major challenge for them in delivering effective reading instruction was providing students challenging, motivating independent learning activities that met their varying needs while they worked with guided reading groups and their EIR group. Therefore, this section details some of the differentiated literacy activities Heather, John, and Linda organized for their students during independent work time. Also provided are other suggestions and resources. With these ideas, you will hopefully feel energized not only to teach your guided reading groups, but also to teach struggling readers in small groups using EIR intervention strategies, just as Heather, John, and Linda did. Figures 7-1 through 7-12 shown here are also available on the DVD as full-size reproducibles. Note that they are discussed throughout the following pages, to show you how they are used in the classroom.

Practicing and Rating My Reading Fluency

Name _____ Date _____

Title _____

I read my story _____ times.

a. My reading rate was: Good 😊 Okay 😐 Could Be Better 🙁

b. My phrasing was: Good 😊 Okay 😐 Could Be Better 🙁

c. My expression was: Good 😊 Okay 😐 Could Be Better 🙁

I want to work on a, b, or c (circle one).

Figure 7-1 Practice and Rating My Reading Fluency

Log for Independent Pleasure Reading

Name _____ Date _____

Book Title	Date	Start page	End page	My ideas are:

Figure 7-2 Log for Independent Pleasure Reading

Concept Map

Book Title _____ Page _____

Name _____ Date _____

Use words or draw pictures with words.

It means:

My connection:

Juicy word:

Sentence:

An example:

Figure 7-3 Concept Map

Cause-Effect Chart

Book _____

Name _____ Date _____

Use words or draw pictures with words.

This happened (Cause)	On page	That made this happen (Effect)	On page	My ideas

Figure 7-4 Cause-Effect Chart

 See the DVD for full-size versions of all the forms in this chapter.

Topic Map

Name _____ Date _____

Use words or draw pictures with words

Food:

Habitat:

My animal (topic) is:

Babies:

Appearance:

Interesting facts:

Figure 7-5 Topic Map

Comparison Chart

Name _____ Books _____

Date _____

	Animal 1	Similar (S) or Different (D)	Animal 2
	Wolf		Coyote
Appearance	90 lbs	D	45 pounds
Food	Little animals	S	Little animals
Habitat	Woods	S	Woods
Babies			
Interesting Facts	Travel in a pack	D	Travel alone

Figure 7-6 Comparison Chart

Fact-Opinion Chart

Name _____ Book Title _____

Idea (sentence)	Page	Fact (F) or Opinion (O)	Why?

Figure 7-7 Fact-Opinion Chart

Narrative Summary Sheet

Name _____ Book Title _____

Summarize the story in complete sentences. You can draw pictures after you write.

Beginning (who, where, problem):

Middle (events):

End (solution):

Author's message:

New Words

Write two words that you did not know or that you found interesting and what you think they mean if you can.

Word	Page	Meaning

Figure 7-8 Narrative Summary Sheet

Summary Sheet for Informational Text

Name _____

Summarize the informational text you read. Write in complete sentences.
You can draw pictures after you write if you wish.

Part 1	Main Idea	Important Details
Part 1		
Part 2		
Part 3		

New Words

Write two words that you did not know or that you found interesting and what you think they mean if you can.

Word	Page	Meaning

Figure 7-9 Summary Sheet for Informational Text

Note-Taking Sheet on Comprehension Monitoring

Name _____ Date _____

Word or idea that confused me	Page	Notes

Figure 7-10 Note-Taking Sheet on Comprehension Monitoring

Note-Taking Sheet for an Oral Book Report

Name _____ Date _____

A. Beginning: Characters, Setting, Problem

B. Events

C. Solution to Problem

D. Author's Message

Share Your Ideas

1. Tell about a part you liked and why.

2. Tell how this is like your life and why.

New Words

Write two words that you did not know or that you found interesting and what you think they mean if you can.

Word	Page	Meaning

Figure 7-11 Note-Taking Sheet for an Oral Book Report

Note-Taking Sheet for Vocabulary and High-Level Questions to Discuss at a Book Club

Question Sheet for Narrative Books

Book:

Names:

Write two juicy questions about the story (why, how, what do you think?)

1.

2.

Share Your Ideas

1. Tell about a part you liked and why.

2. Tell how this is like your life and why.

New Words

Write two words that you did not know or that you found interesting and what you think they mean if you can.

Figure 7-12 Note-Taking Sheet for Vocabulary and High-Level Questions to Discuss at a Book Club

Independent Activities in Heather's Classroom

Independent activities that Heather structures for her students include working independently, with a partner, or in a small-group on reading, rereading for fluency, writing in a journal, writing on an open response sheet, talking with others about what they have read or written about in their reading, and going on the computer to read or gather new information. Early in the year, students many need to draw and write a response. As soon as they are able, Heather has them focus on writing as opposed to drawing. Examples for different days (A–D) from Heather's classroom include the following:

Example A

▶ Write a postcard about what you learned about homes around the world. You will take your postcard home to share with a family member.

▶ Talk with a partner about the words *moral to the story* and then in your journal, write in your own words what this means.

▶ Write in your journal about the moral in the fable about the crow and the pitcher (questions are on the whiteboard).

▶ Talk with a partner about solving problems like the problem the crow had to solve and then write about this in your journal.

Example B

▶ Read a new story with a moral or lesson in it.

▶ Write a story map on the new story you were given to read (see Narrative Summary Sheet, Figure 7-8). Include the moral (author's message).

▶ Share this idea map with a partner and make additions or changes after sharing.

▶ Read for pleasure from a book of your choice.

Example C

▶ Reread the text on animal teeth for fluency (see Practicing and Rating My Reading Fluency, Figure 7-1).

▶ Answer the questions in the *Weekly Reader* on animal teeth.

▶ Choose another book on the back table to read about another animal and its teeth.

▶ Read for pleasure from a book of your choice (see Log for Independent Pleasure Reading, Figure 7-2).

- ◗ Finish summarizing the informational text on frogs (from whole-group lesson) (see Summary Sheet for Informational Text, Figure 7-9).

- ◗ Write about whether you would like to be a tadpole or a frog and share what you wrote with a partner.

- ◗ In your journal, write about "luck" from the small-group story on the frog who saved the tadpoles (average group), or if in EIR, write about helping others (follow-up to *Herman the Helper*).

- ◗ Work on a research report on a mammal of your choosing (see Topic Map, Figure 7-5).

- ◗ Read for pleasure from a book of your choice.

On other days during the year, Heather also has students do research reports with a partner on a variety of topics of their choosing or on topics related to their social studies or science curriculum. In addition, she gives students questions about stories they read in their guided reading groups and has them engage in student-led discussions (see Note-taking Sheet for Vocabulary and High-Level Questions form in Figure 7-12.).

Independent Activities in John's Classroom

John organizes the independent activities so they meet the varying needs of all the students in his class. He has students work with partners and alone. During independent activities, students might write summaries and responses to stories they've read as a class and on their own, as well as research topics of interest, record in their reading log what they have read, and of course read and reread favorite stories. An example of the activities students might have done during reading block in John's class would be:

- ◗ Complete a summary that they started in whole group on the story about the crab that was looking for a new home.

- ◗ Reread their small-group story for fluency.

- ◗ Write a summary in their own words on the story they read in their small group (see a sample Narrative Summary Sheet, Figure 7-8).

- ◗ Read from their book boxes and write on their reading log what they read for the day (see a sample Log for Independent Pleasure Reading, Figure 7-2).

John is constantly assessing to see whether the activities are challenging the students to become more fluent and thoughtful readers. He does this by watching the students closely as they engage in the various activities, as well as by reading and reviewing their work on an ongoing basis.

Independent Activities in Linda's Classroom

Linda has found that informational texts excite and motivate her first graders. Therefore, many of the independent activities involve students finding information in books, reading books on the same topic, and documenting what they have learned. Of course, the independent activities also include reading and then writing and talking in response to what students read. Students typically have three or four different activities to work on during their independent work time. Examples from different days (A–C) include the following:

Example A

▶ Summarize the story we read today in your response journal (see Figure 7-8).

▶ Find juicy words from your independent reading and write them on sticky notes that you put in your book. After sharing, students write about some of these words (see Concept Map, Figure 7-3).

▶ Write about things you learned in your *National Geographic* books (see Topic Map, Figure 7-5).

▶ Do pleasure reading (see Log for Independent Pleasure Reading form, Figure 7-2).

Example B

▶ Write in your own words what you learned about sharks (see Topic Map, Figure 7-5).

▶ Do more reading about sharks and write down three interesting facts (see Topic Map, Figure 7-5).

▶ Do pleasure reading (see Log, Figure 7-2).

Example C

▶ Write about a time you felt snug like the character in our story today and share your ideas with a partner.

▶ Read in *National Geographic* books and look for juicy words to write down on sticky notes to share later (students could use Concept Map, Figure 7-3).

▶ Read for pleasure (see Log, Figure 7-2).

All three teachers provide challenging learning activities, during independent work time. They have students engage in

▶ Independent and partner work related to high-level talk and writing in response to what they are reading

▶ Student-led discussions of book club books

▶ Researching and writing reports based on books of their own choosing

▶ Independent reading for pleasure from books of their own choosing. (By the middle of first grade, when most students have cracked the code and can read on their own, they should read for about 30 minutes a day for pleasure.)

It is important to remember to watch students closely to see if the independent work is both motivating and challenging. Having students choose different ways to respond to the books they've read helps with this endeavor. It also fosters independence and responsibility.

More Suggestions for Challenging Independent Activities

Independent work time can be one of the most academically powerful junctures of the school day, because it's when students actually practice being the motivated, self-regulated learners we want them to be. The following additional activities sufficiently engage and challenge first graders so they are less likely to go off-task into unproductive behavior. Making independent time work well is crucial because independence is one goal we're after—self-regulated, motivated learners.

What factors prevent first graders from learning to read and learning to enjoy reading? Low-level tasks are one major factor. Research by Pressley and colleagues (2003) found that teaching behaviors that undermined academic motivation in primary-grade classrooms included tasks with low-task difficulty in which students were asked to complete activities that were too easy, required low cognitive effort, and demanded little of them (80). Also students in these classrooms were given activities that were uninspiring, boring, simplistic, and lacked excitement or provided stimulation to students.

In my many visits to first-grade classrooms over the ten years I worked with schools on schoolwide reading improvement (Taylor et al. 2005; Taylor 2010c), I often saw students engaged in primarily low-level tasks during independent work time. Typically, students in these classrooms were completing worksheets or workbook pages, coloring, cutting and pasting, and rereading stories more times than were warranted. Also, these activities often could be completed in much less time than the time allowed, which only compounded the likelihood that students dawdled, got off-task, chatted with students near them, or wandered around the room.

At the other end of the spectrum, on my schools visits, I also went into classrooms in which students were participating in many tasks requiring high-level thinking and collaboration during independent work time. The levels of student engagement and the numbers of happy faces and excited eyes in these classrooms as compared to classrooms with less-motivating activities were striking. Students typically had three or four activities to complete that kept them meaningfully engaged and working at a continuous, efficient pace. With enough to do and with interesting things to work on, they did not get off-task. Most importantly, they appeared to be happy learners.

These observations are supported by research of Pressley and colleagues (2003) on tasks that enhanced academic motivation in primary-grade classrooms. They found that teachers had motivated learners when they engaged them in cooperative learning and high-order, critical, and creative thinking. For example, in grade 1, students might discuss a book in a student-led book club in which high-level questions were written on a discussion card by the teacher, or two students might read about, collaboratively write, and co-present a research report on an animal of their own choosing. These teachers also used engaging and interesting texts that piqued students' curiosity, got them excited about their learning, and involved them in excellent literature.

Independent work time activities to engage students and advance their literacy abilities are provided. Independent student response sheets that go with some of these suggestions are on the DVD (Figures 7-1 to 7-12).

Activities That Support Word Recognition

▶ To reinforce students' knowledge of symbol-sound correspondence that you have recently taught in guided reading groups, have them complete word sorts with a partner. For example, if you have recently taught a group that there are two common sounds for *a*, the short and long sounds, you could have them sort words containing /a/ with the CVC and CVCe patterns. To get practice reading words containing particular phonic elements, students should read the words that have been sorted.

Suggested Professional Reading. See sequences for word sorts in *Words Their Way* by Bear et al., 2007, pages 375–93.

▶ To reinforce students' knowledge of symbol-sound correspondence that you have recently taught in guided reading groups, have them write words that fall into various word families with a partner. A skilled reader (volunteer, educational assistant, older student helper) should check words generated (e.g., so that *bight* for *bite* is not written under words with the *-ight* pattern). To get practice reading words containing particular phonic elements, students should read the words they have generated.

See words for word families in *Words Their Way* by Bear et al., 2007, pages 375–93.

▶ Have students work with a partner or small group to generate words in a Making Words activity in which the directions have been written on a card by the teacher. To get practice reading words containing particular phonic elements, students should read words generated and sort words into word families.

For more on Making Words, see *Phonics They Use: Words for Reading and Writing*, 5th ed., Cunningham, 2009.

▶ If your school's spelling curriculum uses weekly spelling lists and tests, have students practice spelling misspelled words from their weekly spelling lists after you have given students a pretest and they have self-corrected misspelled words. Word lists should be differentiated based on students' reading and spelling abilities.

Activities That Support Fluency

▶ With a partner, have students reread stories from their guided reading group or EIR lesson. Students should coach one another on difficult words. See Chapter 3, page 38, for prompts for students to use during partner reading.

For additional suggestions on fluency, see *The Fluent Reader: Oral Reading Strategies for Building Word Recognition, Fluency, and Comprehension*, Rasinski, 2003.

▶ Have students reread stories from their guided reading group or EIR lesson with a volunteer, educational assistant, or older student helper (who coaches as students get stuck on words they cannot decode instantly).

▶ Have students reread stories in their book box. They should list books reread for fluency, and self-rate their fluency on books read (see Figure 7-1).

▶ Have students read new books for pleasure. They should log books they read (see Figure 7-2).

For additional vocabulary suggestions see *Bringing Words to Life: Robust Vocabulary Instruction,* Beck, McKeown, and Kucan, 2002.

Activities That Support Vocabulary

▶ On sticky notes or in a vocabulary journal, have students write down interesting, unknown, or newly learned words that come from the books they are reading. Students can share words and possible meanings with the teacher in a whole- or small-group lesson or by turning their vocabulary journal in to teacher, or with a volunteer, educational assistant, or older classroom helper.

▶ Have students complete a concept map or web of juicy words identified by their teacher from books they are reading (see Figure 7-3).

For more suggestions to teach comprehension skills and strategies, see *Comprehension Shouldn't Be Silent,* Kelley and Clausen-Grace, 2007, and *QAR Now,* Raphael, Highfield, and Au, 2006.

Activities That Support Comprehension: Skills and Strategies

▶ Have students read books to practice comprehension skills and strategies. Examples of open-ended response sheets include the following: cause-effect chart (Figure 7-4), concept map (Figure 7-3), comparison chart (Figure 7-6), fact/opinion chart (Figure 7-7), summary for narrative text (Figure 7-8), summary for informational text (Figure 7-9), comprehension monitoring (Figure 7-10).

▶ Have students write questions as they read or after they are finished reading. Question types include the following: clarifying, interpretive main idea, summary, evaluative/critical literacy.

Activities That Support Comprehension: Learning New Information

Have students:

▶ Read books to learn new information about topics of interest.

▶ Read on the Internet to learn more information.

For more suggestions, see *Reading and Writing Informational Text in the Primary Grades,* Duke and Bennett-Armistead, 2003, and *Informational Text in K–3 Classrooms: Helping Children Read and Write,* Kletsien and Dreher, 2005.

▶ Read books, magazines, and other texts that address social studies and science curriculum. Teachers, the media specialist, or volunteers could locate existing books at the school or purchase books (with school funds, funds from PTA, funds or local businesses) at various reading levels that covered topics in social studies and science curriculum for grade 1.

▶ Prepare and give an oral presentation (Figure 7-11) with a partner, triad, or independently.

▶ Prepare a written report (Figure 7-5 or 7-6). Students could do reports with a partner, triad, or independently. Other topics for writing after reading include: procedures, recounting an event, explanation, or persuasion.

▶ Write down words to share (vocabulary) and write about them (Figure 7-3) after independent reading on topics of interest.

Activities That Support Comprehension: Talk and Writing About Text

Students can work on the following after they have had modeling and coaching lessons from the teacher.

▶ Participate in literature circles—learn routines, read and take notes, share (Figure 7-12).

▶ Respond to literature (Figure 7-11, 7-12).

▶ Prepare and give a book report (Figure 7-11).

Activities That Support Reading for Pleasure

Have students:

▶ Read books from different genre for about 30 minutes a day. After reading, have students complete reading log (Figure 7-2).

▶ Read different books from a favorite author.

▶ Share favorite books in a book sharing club.

▶ Write about favorite books on cards for a book file that other students can look through for book suggestions.

Independent work time is an important component of teachers' overall classroom reading program. Students spend a considerable amount of time working on their own or with others while teachers work with small, guided reading groups. It is crucial that students are actively engaged in interesting, challenging learning activities that meet their needs and move them forward in literacy abilities during this independent work time. However, it is easy for these independent learning activities to become routine, undifferentiated, unnecessary practice, and not motivating or challenging to students. When this happens, it is easy for students to get off-task or spend much more time than is needed on assigned activities. To alleviate these issues, many teachers find that teaching students how to engage in a wide variety of independent activities every so often works well, as does providing students with choice. Additionally, providing students with long-term projects (e.g., author studies, research reports) can also avert some of the routinization of the activities. Furthermore, never underestimate the power of sharing ideas with colleagues about effective independent learning activities.

tips

For more suggestions see *Book Club: A Literature-Based Curriculum.* 2d ed. Raphael, Pardo, and Highfield, 2002.

Moving Forward with Literature Circles, Day, Spiegel, McLellan, and Brown, 2002.

Using Literature to Enhance Content Area Instruction: A Guide for K–5 Teachers, Olness, 2007.

tips

For more suggestions see *What Should I Read Aloud?* Anderson, 2007, and *Literature on the Child*, 7th ed., Galda and Cullinan, 2010.

tips

For more on effective, motivating reading instruction and assessment in general:

Classroom Reading Assessment: Making Sense of What Students Know and Do, Paratore and McCormack, 2007.

Reading Instruction That Works: The Case for Balanced Teaching, 3rd ed., Pressley et al., 2003.

On Solid Ground: Strategies for Teaching Reading K–3, Taberski, 2000.

For more on differentiated reading instruction:
Differentiated Small-Group Reading Lessons, Southall, 2009.

How to Plan Differentiated Reading Instruction: Resources for Grades K–3, Walpole and McKenna, 2009.

8

Creating an EIR Community

• •

Early Intervention in Reading is a powerful approach for accelerating the reading development of children who find learning to read difficult, and in some respects it's easy to implement. The predictable structure, the small-group attention, and the motivating literature at its heart make it something that teachers and children quickly grow to like. However, because it isn't a curriculum but rather a repertoire of teaching strategies, and because any learner who struggles requires teachers to reflect and use considerable skill, I strongly encourage teachers to enlist support along the following three lines.

1. Teachers need to work with colleagues during their first year of teaching EIR lessons.

First and foremost, over many years, I have found that teachers experience more success with their students when they regularly participate in monthly meetings with colleagues to discuss EIR during the first year they are teaching the lessons. Together, teachers can clarify procedures, share successes, and help one another solve problems. Taking on EIR and weaving it in to effective whole-group and small-group instruction amounts to highly differentiated teaching—not an easy thing to achieve.

In a research study on effective reading practices (Taylor, Pearson, Clark, and Walpole 2000), the most effective schools had a collaborative model for delivering reading instruction in which struggling readers received a second, 30-minute

small-group reading intervention each day to accelerate their literacy learning. Therefore, I strongly recommend that classroom teachers, Title 1 and other reading resource teachers, ELL teachers, and special education teachers meet together in these monthly EIR professional learning experiences. Teachers will not solve all of their students' reading problems unless they work collaboratively. Classroom teachers know their students the best and must be part of the solution.

2. Teachers enlist the help from others on scheduling the monthly meetings and sustaining the one-on-one coaching conferences that are an essential piece of EIR.

If numerous teachers are learning about and teaching EIR in the same year, it is extremely helpful if a school has a building facilitator to provide support. This person can take responsibility for securing EIR books and materials, for scheduling professional learning sessions, for establishing the one-on-one coaching component of EIR by aides, volunteers, or older students, and for problem solving as issues arise.

3. Teachers need to reach out to parents/caregivers, so that they can help their children practice reading at home.

Parents have a critical role to play in EIR. Children take their EIR story home at the end of the third day so they can read to their parents. In Figure 8-1 is a Reading at Home sheet for parents to sign. (Note: All the figures in this chapter are supplied as full-sized reproducibles on the DVD). In Figure 8-2, there are coaching prompts for parents to use when listening to their children read. Also, in the supplemental resources on the DVD, there are take-home activities based on the EIR stories that the parents, or an older sibling, other relative, or neighbor, should help their children with at home. Parents should sign the EIR at-home sheets and have their children bring them back to school.

To introduce these activities to parents, a sample letter you can send home explaining EIR is provided in Figure 8-3. Also, at the beginning of the school year, you can invite parents to an "EIR Party," perhaps at the school's back-to-school-night event, in which you explain the materials that will be coming home and the importance of parents' involvement in these activities. You can demonstrate the coaching prompts for parents at this time. Also, you may want to show parents a video of yourself coaching children in their EIR group. Children can come along to the party and eat cookies to make it seem like a festive event.

For parents who can't make it to school, you can send home a video of yourself reading with their child and coaching as the child is stuck on difficult

Reading at Home Sheet

Date _____

_____ **has read the book**
(student's name)

_____ **to me _____ times.**
(book name)

Comments:_____
_____
_____
_____
_____
_____
_____
_____

_____
(parent's/caregiver's signature)

Figure 8-1 Reading at Home Sheet

Tips for Reading with Beginning Readers at Home

In EIR, teachers help children learn to depend on themselves to figure out hard words. To work on this at home, try one of the following prompts or tips when a young reader gets stuck or makes a mistake:

1. Wait and see if they work it out.
2. Say, "Try that again."
3. Say, "Look at the picture."
4. Say, "Think about what would make sense."
5. Say, "Sound it out."

If the word is a hard one, you may want to tell the child the word. But if the word is an easy one, try one or more of these tips listed before you give the child the word.

Figure 8-2 Tips for Reading with Beginning Readers at Home

Parent/Guardian Information Letter

Dear Parent/Guardian,

To help maximize your child's success in reading, we are using supplementary reading lessons called Early Intervention in Reading (EIR). EIR will help your child by using a different approach to experience reading success. We are excited about it!

We want to emphasize that we really need your involvement. How can you help? Watch for a book and/or take-home activities your child will bring home. Be sure to listen to your child read the story and help with the take-home activities. Return the take-home activity with your signature. Research shows, *"Kids who read the most, read the best!"*

This is the way we teach EIR:

1. The teacher reads the book to the group.
2. The teacher guides students as they read the story and then discuss it.
3. Three to five words are selected by the teacher to work on decoding.
4. Children write a sentence about the story.
5. The child practices reading the book at home.

Remember: Listen to your child read the book and assist with the take-home activities. Please help your child return the completed take-home activities page with your signature.

Thank you for your continued support as we work together to help your child have success in reading.

Sincerely,

Figure 8-3 Parent Information Letter

words. One teacher reported taping each child in November and May and then giving the recording to the parents at the end of the year. Another strategy teachers have used for involving parents is inviting them to school to see EIR lessons in action.

Overview of Monthly EIR Meetings

Now let's look at a yearly framework for professional learning sessions that include how often to have meetings, sample agendas, and suggestions for what to address throughout the year. See Table 8-1.

At monthly meetings of about an hour, teachers learning to teach EIR lessons can work together to gain expertise and confidence about doing these intervention lessons, honing their abilities to coach children to use word-recognition strategies, to depend on themselves, and to pose questions about the EIR stories that lead to high-level, comprehension-building responses. Swapping successes, trials, classroom management ideas, and authentic independent activities—teachers can support one another around so many teaching issues.

Begin the meetings in August or September and continue through May. If it's hard to find an hour once a month, you can meet for shorter times over several days during the month. In the first 10 to 15 minutes, the group can focus

Monthly Meeting Overview

August/September	Review Chapters 1, 2, 3, and 7 Discuss instructional procedures and watch video clips on the DVD that go with Chapter 3 Review fall assessments Prepare for October meeting
October	Status report on EIR teaching (discuss how your EIR groups are going; review procedures as questions arise) Review video-sharing procedures Discuss one-on-one coaching Review EIR procedures Prepare for November meeting
November	Status report on EIR teaching Status report of one-on-one coaching Review video viewing procedures Discuss grade-level procedures Engage in video sharing Prepare for December meeting
December	Status report on EIR teaching Discuss one-on-one coaching Group Activity: Book Lesson Share Grade-level procedures Group Activity: Practice Making Words Video sharing Prepare for January meeting
January	Status report on EIR teaching Coaching for comprehension Status report on one-on-one coaching Grade-level procedures Video viewing/sharing Prepare for February meeting
February	Status of children's progress Grade-level procedures Group Activity: Sentence Writing Discuss transition phase Video sharing Prepare for March meeting
March	Status of children's progress Discuss transition phase Video sharing Prepare for April meeting
April	Status of children's progress Grade-level procedures Review spring assessment procedures
May (if time permits, or at a grade-level meeting)	Status of children's progress Discuss results of assessments Review year and discuss plans for next year

Table 8-1 *Monthly Meeting Overview*

on sharing ideas and concerns related to EIR lessons. Teachers can also take about 30 to 40 minutes to review and discuss grade-level procedures (See Figure 3-1) and the videos clips of effective practice found on the DVD. By November, I encourage teachers to bring their own video segments of teaching EIR lessons.

August

In August, read and discuss Chapters 1 and 2 with the group of teachers in your school who are participating in the EIR professional learning sessions. You may also want to read and discuss Chapter 7, which includes details about fitting EIR into your daily literacy block and making sure your independent work activities are challenging, motivating, and engaging so you can focus your attention on the students in your guided reading groups or EIR lessons.

September

Additionally, in August or early September, you should begin to review the EIR procedures in Chapter 3. During the September and October meetings, go through the three-day EIR routines for the first time in detail. Also, during monthly meetings, you can revisit certain aspects of the EIR procedures as questions arise.

October

Sometimes teachers report uneasiness about "doing the EIR procedures correctly" and want to delay getting started. However, I always tell teachers not to worry if they are doing things "just right" at first; they will get better at using EIR strategies over time. What is important is to get started with EIR lessons as close to October 1 as possible. Most children who will benefit from EIR need the intervention all year. Students should have the opportunity to be a part of reading intervention lessons that make them feel successful as soon as possible before feelings of discouragement about reading set in.

November

Beginning in November, I recommend you incorporate video sharing into your monthly EIR meetings. To do this, teachers take turns bringing in a 5- to 8-minute video clip of their EIR teaching to share and discuss. These video-sharing experiences give teachers the opportunity to reflect on and discuss their practice. So often, professional development focuses on curriculum lessons tied to a teacher's manual or the proper use of new materials. Teachers are rarely given the opportunity, with the help of colleagues, to think, talk about, and enhance their own teaching practices.

The focus of the video sharing should be:

▶ What the children are doing well or the strengths they are demonstrating in the EIR lesson

▶ What the teacher is doing well to foster strategy use, independence, and success in the children

▶ What else the teacher might have done to foster strategy use, independence, and success.

Through EIR ongoing professional learning sessions, you will improve your coaching abilities. As you focus on coaching and work at it collaboratively, you are reminded that coaching children to become independent is not easy. However, you also learn that coaching is something you can master, with the end result of having more children in your classrooms reading well by the end of the school year. Video-sharing procedures are described in greater detail later in this chapter (also see in Figure 8-4.) A sign-up sheet is in Figure 8-5.

Suggested agendas for the year are detailed in the next few pages. I suggest you read through them now as a way to get an idea of what a year of EIR professional learning might look like. Then, use the monthly Agenda pages to organize and forward your EIR work and learning.

Agendas for Monthly Meetings

● ●

In the following section, a yearly framework for monthly meetings, including aspects of the EIR you might focus on during certain months, a structure for sharing and discussing progress and concerns, as well as protocols for viewing and sharing videos are presented. All these figures are on the DVD.

September Meeting (70–75 min.)

Recommended activities for professional learning in September include:

Review Chapters 1, 2, and 3 (10–15 min.)

First, in September, talk about any remaining questions or issues you have related to Chapters 1 and 2. You may also wish to discuss Chapter 7 because it covers fitting EIR into your daily schedule and offers ideas for productive independent work for other students while you are working with your EIR group.

Discuss Instructional Procedures in Chapter 3 (35–40 min.)

Carefully work through Chapter 3. This chapter covers Grade 1 EIR routines. Also, watch the related video clips on the DVD.

Review Fall Assessments (20 min.)

Review the fall assessment procedures described in Chapter 6. Select passages from an informal reading inventory that you will all use in the fall assessments to determine which students need EIR lessons.

Prepare for October Meeting (5 min.)

Briefly review what needs to be done before the October meeting:

▶ You should have your EIR children identified. Don't worry if you aren't quite sure about your placement decisions. You can ask questions in October and make changes then.

▶ You should start your EIR lessons before you meet in October and as close to October 1 as possible. You will get a lot more out of the October meeting if you have already started to teach EIR lessons. You should jot down notes on this instruction so you have a chance to share experiences and to get questions answered at the October meeting.

Often, teachers say they aren't ready to get started yet, but I tell them to simply "take the plunge" and realize that you will be getting better at teaching EIR lessons as the year moves along. The best way to learn about EIR instructional strategies is to start teaching EIR lessons. Good luck!

October Meeting (65–70 min.)

This month you will continue to learn and talk about procedures in grade-level groups. Additionally, you need to prepare for video sharing, which should begin in November. You also need to make sure the one-on-one reading coaching will be in place soon if it's not already.

Status Report on EIR Teaching (10 min.)

Take turns reporting on how things have gone so far with the initial teaching of EIR lessons.

Review Video-Sharing Procedures (20 min.)

Each person should bring one video to share in November, December, or January and a second in February, March, or April. Share one or two videos each month. To learn about video sharing, see Figure 8-4 below.

The basic approach to video sharing was developed for the EIR Professional Development Program but has also been used with success in other teacher professional development venues (Taylor 2010c). Each video-sharing segment should take no more than 15 minutes.

Prior to coming to your study group, do the following:

1. Videotape the lesson segment you selected. It should be 5 minutes long.

2. Answer the following three video-sharing questions based on your video:

▶ What were things the children were able to do related to your focus area? What things were going well?

▶ What was the teacher doing to help children develop and be successful related to your focus area?

▶ What else could have been done to foster development and success related to your focus area?

When you share the video at an EIR session, do the following:

1. Share 1 minute of background about the lesson.

2. Tell the group something you would like their help with and thus want them to pay attention to while watching the video clip.

Engaging in Video Sharing

The basic approach to video sharing was developed for the Early Intervention in Reading (EIR) Professional Development Program but has also been used in other teacher professional development venues. Each video-sharing segment should take no more than 15 minutes. Focus on students' strategy use, independence, and success.

Prior to coming to your study group, do the following:

a. Videotape the lesson segment you selected. It should be 5 minutes long.

b. Answer the following three video-sharing questions based on your video:

▶ What were things the children were able to do related to your focus area? What things were going well?

▶ What was the teacher doing to help children develop and be successful related to your focus area?

▶ What else could have been done to foster development and success related to your focus area?

When you share the video at an EIR session, do the following:

1. Share 1 minute of background about the lesson.

2. Tell the group something you would like their help with.

3. View the video with the group.

4. Break into groups of three to review the three video-sharing questions. Take notes on things the children did well, things the teacher in the clip did well in getting children to develop and experience success related to the focus area, and offer suggestions for things that might have been done differently to help the children develop and experience success related to the focus area.

5. Discuss the video clip as a larger group. (View the video again if group feels it needs to.) The facilitator will ask the three video-sharing questions to the group. Members from the groups of three can share points that they wish to share. Notes from small groups should be given to the teacher who brought the video clip of her teaching.

6. The teacher who brought the clip should ask for their ideas related to with item 2 above.

Remember, this is first and foremost a learning activity in which colleagues are helping one another improve their skills as coaches. At an EIR session, sign up for a topic—one part of one day's lesson (see Figure 8–5).

Figure 8-4 Engaging in Video Sharing

3. View the video with the group.

4. Break into groups of three to review the three video-sharing questions. Take notes on things the children did well, things the teacher in the clip did well in getting children to develop related to the focus area and to experience success related to this focus area, and offer suggestions for things that might have been done differently to help the children develop and experience success related to the focus area.

5. Discuss the video clip as a larger group. (View the video again if group feels it needs to.) The facilitator will ask the three video-sharing questions to the group. Members from the groups of three can share points that they wish to share. Notes from small groups should be given to the teacher who brought the video clip of her teaching.

6. The teacher who brought the clip should ask for their ideas related to with item 2.

Remember, this is first and foremost a learning activity in which colleagues are helping one another improve their abilities as coaches. At an EIR session, sign up to show a video clip of their teaching for a specific topic—one part of one day's lesson. (See form in Figure 8-5.)

People should sign up for the video sharing in October (see Figure 8-5). If you have more than six teachers in your group, break into groups of from three to five members for the video sharing part of the meeting. With six members in a video-sharing group, you would watch two videos a month. With three members in a video-sharing group, you would watch one video a month. Everyone should share their first video in November, December, or January, and a second video in February, March, or April.

Figure 8-5 Video Sharing—Sign-Up Sheet for Grade 1

Video Sharing—Sign-Up Sheet for Grade 1

Month	Teacher	Description of Video
November		Teacher models word-recognition strategies as she reads book on Day 1
		Sound Box activity
		Sentence writing
December		Teacher coaches or takes oral reading check as children reread old stories
		Teachers coaches as children read story on Day 2
		Coaching for comprehension
January		Teacher coaches as children read story on Day 3
		Making Words activity
		Coaching for comprehension
February		Teacher coaches as children read story on Days 2 or 3
		Sentence writing
March		Coaching for comprehension
		Transition
April		Coaching for comprehension
		Transition

Discuss One-on-One Coaching (10 min.)

Discuss the status of the one-on-one coaching piece of EIR or the plans for getting this component in place as soon as possible. One-on-one coaches might be educational assistants, classroom volunteers, or older students who are classroom helpers who receive training on how to be a coach. (See the section on training coaches later in this chapter and in Figure 8-6.)

To get maximum results with EIR, one-on-one coaching needs to occur on a regular basis. Children need the opportunity to practice reading with no other child next to them who calls out a word they don't know. Also, individual children need the chance to show themselves what they are able to do on their own. Even if you are not responsible for training the one-on-one coaches, you should look through the information presented on this topic in this chapter so you understand the training the coaches have received. Also, as the classroom teacher, you need to supervise the one-on-one coaches and give constructive feedback as needed.

Review of EIR Procedures (20–25 min.)

By grade level, you should use notes you have kept to raise questions about teaching EIR lessons so far and to get help from members in your group in answering these questions. You may want to return to the section in Chapter 3 on grade-level routines to answer questions.

You may find it helpful to consider the following observations I have about EIR lessons and students in October.

▶ When I observe teachers and children in EIR lessons in October, I am struck by how much patience is required of the teacher at this time of the year in particular. Realizing that the children still don't grasp the alphabetic principle or the tracking of print, you need to work hard to keep the children focused so they can learn both of these things.

▶ Often, children who are doing well at this time of the year are simply memorizing their stories. This is okay because they are having success with print. Also, it is unlikely that they can "read their EIR stories with their eyes shut." During their reading practice, their eyes are gluing to the print and they are starting to grasp the alphabetic principle. As they get stuck on a word, ask them to think about the story and to look at the first letter. Ask them to check to see if the word they come up with makes sense. Model letter-by-letter decoding and decoding by onset and rime.

▶ If a child is having a hard time catching on, you will have to do more of the tracking and rereading for him. However, insist that the child is attending and trying to track. Have the child track and reread after you have modeled this. Ask questions like, "Point to the word *sat* that we just read. Does it look like *sat*?" Model how /s/ /a/ /t/ is /sat/. Continue to model letter-by-letter decoding, decoding by onset and rime, and checking to see if words that are decoded make sense in the story.

▶ Review and discuss the following video clips related to modeling and coaching in word recognition: Videos 2 and 8.

Remember that it helps children as they are writing for sounds to actually say the words as they are trying to write them. (See Videos 10 and 14.)

Prepare for November Meeting (5 min.)

For the November meeting, one or two people per small group should bring in short video clips to share of predetermined segments of EIR lessons. (See sign-up sheet in Figure 8-5.) A segment would be Step 1, 2, or 3, or 4 of Day 1, 2, or 3.

November Meeting (60–75 min.)

Status Report on EIR Teaching (10 min.)

Share successes and continued questions you have about EIR teaching.

Status Report on One-on-One Coaching (5 min.)

Discuss how this is working for your and your students. Discuss any scheduling issues or concerns.

Review Video Sharing Procedures (5 min.)

Discuss any questions or concerns about video sharing, logistics and feelings you may have had about the video taping.

Discuss Grade-Level Procedures (20 min.)

By now you are probably feeling more comfortable with the EIR routine. However, in November it is important to consider your timing in EIR lessons. You want to be sure you are getting to all of the parts of a lesson. Also, you want to be moving toward the goal of only spending three days on a book. Discuss strategies for getting through all parts of a lesson. If there are parts of the EIR routine that you want to review, return to the relevant sections of Chapter 3 and the corresponding video clips.

Observations I typically have in November include the following:

▶ Don't worry if the children are still memorizing their stories. As stories get longer and harder in EIR Level B, memorizing will be more difficult and thus less likely. Also, children will start decoding the words in their stories as they begin to grasp the alphabetic principle.

▶ You should not expect children to recognize the words in their EIR stories as sight words in isolation. Drilling on sight words is not part of the EIR program.

▶ I find that most first-grade children in EIR are tracking by Thanksgiving, and this is always an exciting sign of progress. Don't worry, however, that about a quarter of your EIR students will still not be able to track by the end of November. It will take them a little longer, but it will come.

Video Sharing (15–30 min.)

Share one or two videos, depending on the size of your group.

Many teachers are nervous about the video sharing, but they also find that it gets a lot easier by the second time around. In May, on EIR evaluations, many teachers state that the video sharing was one of the most valuable parts of EIR professional learning sessions. So hang in there with the video-sharing experience.

Prepare for December Meeting (5 min.)

For the December meeting, one or two people (depending on the size of your group) should be bringing in short video clips to share predetermined segments of EIR lessons.

December Meeting (65–80 min.)

Status Report on EIR Teaching (10 min.)

By December the EIR procedure should seem like second nature. Therefore, it is a good time to reflect on your coaching for comprehension. Keep a list of the questions you ask your students, jot down notes on your questioning practices, and bring them to share at January meeting.

The following questions should get you thinking about your questioning and coaching for comprehension. Take a few min. to reflect on your answers.

▶ Are you asking follow-up questions to get a child to clarify what they are saying or to elaborate on their ideas?

▶ Are you giving a child enough wait time?

▶ Are you coaching quiet children (e.g., those who like to say, "I don't know") to talk instead of just moving on to another child?

▶ Are you asking questions that are based on a concept in the story but that leave the story behind and instead relate to children's lives (e.g., What could you do beside watch TV if you woke up early like Milton in *Milton the Early Riser*?)?

▶ Are your questions thought provoking and meaningful to the children (e.g., after reading *The Carrot Seed,* "Tell about something you did that some people thought you wouldn't be able to do. How did you feel?" Why is this more thought provoking than, "Tell about something you planted. How did you feel?")?

Status Report on One-on-One Coaching (5 min.)

It is very important that this component of EIR be up and running. If possible, try to observe your one-on-one coaches so you can give them feedback.

tips

By now, or in January at the latest, you should be using Making Words strategies instead of the Sound Boxes activity with your children on Day 1. Often children hate to give up the Sound Box activity because it is something they are good at. But as they are advancing, they will be getting more out of Making Words than Sound Boxes, so it is time to make the switch. To review the procedures for Making Words, return to the section on Making Words in Chapter 3 and watch Grade 1 Videos 6 and 7 on the DVD.

Group Activity: Book Lesson Share (10 min.)

Take books you will be using in future EIR lessons and with a partner, generate some good coaching for comprehension questions. Share these with the larger group.

Grade-level Procedures (15 min.)

Most children in EIR groups will still need to use their finger to track at this point in the school year, so remind them to do this if they aren't. Later in the spring, however, most children will naturally quit tracking. At this later point in time, you may need to encourage children to quit tracking with their fingers if they are using it as a crutch.

Group Activity: Practice Making Words (10 min.)

Practice the Making Words activities as a group. Remember to include the word-sorting component and to stress the importance of transferring knowledge about word families to independent reading.

Video Sharing (15–30 min.)

Engage in video sharing.

Prepare for January Meeting (2 min.)

For the January meeting, two people per small group should be bringing in short video clips to share of a predetermined piece of an EIR lesson. Remember to bring in the notes from your coaching for comprehension. Also, if you are meeting in late January, you should read about and discuss the transition to independent reading phase in Chapter 5 at this time instead of waiting until a late February meeting.

January Meeting (70–75 min.)

Status Report on EIR Teaching (5–10 min.)

Briefly report on successes you are seeing with your students—even after the holiday break!

Coaching for Comprehension (10 min.)

At the December meeting, questions were presented to help you focus on your questioning and coaching for comprehension. Discuss your notes and anything you learned about your practice from focusing on these questions.

▶ Are you asking follow-up questions to get a child to clarify what they are saying or to elaborate on their ideas?

▶ Are you giving a child enough wait time?

▶ Are you working with quiet children who like to say, "I don't know," instead of just moving on to another child?

▶ Are you asking questions that are based on a concept in the story but that leave the story behind and instead related to children's lives (e.g., What could you do beside watch TV if you woke up early like Milton in *Milton the Early Riser*)?

▶ Are your questions thought provoking and meaningful to the children (e.g., after reading *The Carrot Seed*, "Tell about something you did that some people thought you wouldn't be able to do. How did you feel?" Why is this more thought provoking than, "Tell about something you planted. How did you feel?")?

Status Report on One-on-One Coaching (5 min.)

In December, you hopefully found the time to observe your one-on-one coaches and to give them feedback. Discuss issues and concerns.

Grade-Level Procedures (20 min.)

Share successes and brainstorm solutions to concerns regarding Making Words activities. Do this very briefly if you need to move on to a discussion of the transition to independent reading phase of EIR lessons (see February meeting).

At this time of year, I always notice that many first-grade children aren't paying much attention to the meaning of the text when they stop to decode words they don't instantly recognize. This is a typical reaction since much of their cognitive capacity is focused on sounding out the word, something that they have just recently caught on to. However, as a coach, you need to keep reminding children to think about what makes sense in the story as they are trying to decode a word. If they do this, it will make their sounding out a much easier task.

Video Viewing/Sharing (30 min.)

Watch Video 16 (15 min.). The students are engaged in transition reading. Notice how the teacher coaches the children to think about the meaning of the story to help them decode.

Discuss the coaching you do to get children to think about meaning as they are decoding in light of the videos you just saw and in light of your students' success or lack of success at this point in time in using this strategy.

Engage in video sharing (15 min.). Also fill out a new video-sharing sheet for February through April. (See Figure 8-5.)

Prepare for February Meeting (5 minutes)

For the February meeting, two people per small group should bring in short video clips to share of a predetermined piece of an EIR lesson. Also, in Chapter 5 read about *transition to independent reading* that begins in February at the latest and come to the February meeting ready to discuss.

February Meeting (60–80 min.)

Status of Children's Progress (5–10 min.)

I often say to EIR teachers that I love February because by this time they are usually very excited about their students' progress in reading.

However, don't feel discouraged if some of your students are still having some difficulty catching on. Typically about one-quarter to one-third of the children in grade 1 EIR take until April or even May to really catch on to the alphabetic principle.

Briefly report on successes you are seeing with your students.

Grade-level Procedures (15 min.)

At this time of year you really need to help your grade 1 children get used to the idea of being flexible with their vowel sounds. Keep saying to them, "Try one vowel sound, and if that doesn't work, try another" (short or long). Often, children overrely on using the short vowel sound. This is a typical reaction since they have been working so hard to master the short vowel sounds.

Many grade 1 children will benefit more from *writing their own sentence* at this time of the year than writing a group sentence. To review the procedure for independent sentence writing, look at Day 2, Step 4 and Day 3, Step 4 in Chapter 3. An important concept with independent sentence writing in EIR lessons is that you are helping children refine their phonemic awareness as well as their phonics knowledge. It is important to have each child share his or her sentence with you so you can pick out just one or two words to bring to the child's attention in which not all sounds in the word were represented or the sounds were in the wrong order.

Group Activity: Sentence Writing (10 min.)

Discuss your plans pertaining to individual sentence writing. If some of you have already had your children write independent sentences, you may wish to share your experiences to help others.

Discuss Transition Phase (15 min.)

You should begin to transition to independent reading with most of your EIR students in February (or sooner if you feel they are ready). Review the procedures in Chapter 5. If you have started with the transition phase, discuss how it is going.

Video Sharing (15–30 min.)

Engage in video sharing.

Prepare for March Meeting (2 min.)

Be prepared to discuss how the transition phase of the EIR is going for your students and you. You may want to discuss your students' successes, and struggles, as well as the logistics of the transition phase.

March Meeting (50–75 min.)

Status of Children's Progress (5–10 min.)

Briefly report on successes you are seeing with your students.

Discuss Transition Phase (25–30 min.)

By now in grade 1, you should be in the independent reading phase of EIR lessons. Talk with one another about logistics, frustrations, and successes related to having children read independently the first time they open a book. Also, discuss your children's attempts at independent reading.

The transition phase of EIR with its focus on independent (e.g., cold) reading is harder for children and teachers for a number of reasons. The children are often not experiencing quite as much success as they did with the guided, group reading. But they will get better at independent reading, and this is what they need to be doing to become on-grade-level readers. Also, it is harder for teachers to manage the other children in an EIR group when they are working with just two students at a time. Don't forget to use the independent activities ideas from Chapter 7.

Also, reflect as a group on the following: *Many teachers report that they like the opportunity to work with just two children at a time. They say it really helps them understand a child's strengths and weaknesses.*

Video Sharing (15–30 min.)

Engage in video sharing.

Prepare for April Meeting (5 min.)

Before the next meeting, read through the section in Chapter 6 on spring assessments. At the April meeting, you should review spring assessment procedures and answer any questions members of the group may have.

April Meeting (50–65 min.)

Status of Children's Progress (5–10 min.)

Briefly report on successes you are seeing with your students.

Grade-level Procedures (20–25 min.)

Share ideas and concerns. Discuss your successes, problems, and questions pertaining to the transition phase of the EIR program and to children's attempts at transition (independent) reading. Discuss plans for working with struggling readers in the next school year.

Review Spring Assessment Procedures (25–30 min.)

Review the steps for completing the assessments in Chapter 6. Select the passages you will all use from an informal reading inventory. Typically, you should do the assessments during the first two weeks of May before things get really wild at the end of the school year.

Prepare for May Meeting (2 min.)

Be prepared to discuss your assessments and your overall reflections about the year, plus plans for next year.

May Meeting (50–65 min.)

Status of Children's Progress

Share your major successes. How many students will no longer need EIR? How many will require basic EIR next year?

Discuss Results of Assessments

Discuss how students did on the assessments and which assessments provided you with the most information. Were there any surprises (e.g., did some students whom you thought would do well—not do well? Did some students do much better than you expected?)?

Review Year and Discuss Plans for Next Year

Training One-on-One Coaches

The one-on-one coaching component of EIR is a very important piece, but one that sometimes gets overlooked simply because it can be difficult to put in place if people are not readily available to read with students everyday. However, the students make much better progress in reading if they have a chance every day, or as close to every day as possible, to practice reading their newest EIR story with a person who has been trained in how to coach, not tell them words, as they get stuck. Also, in this one-on-one situation, children get to demonstrate to themselves their decoding abilities and don't have the pressure of another child sitting next to them calling out a word before they do.

Celia Huxley, the teacher we saw on the video and an EIR trainer, developed the material in this section to train coaches. She has used it successfully with instructional aides and parent volunteers.

Training Others to Be One-on One Coaches

The following is an agenda (also in Figure 8-6) that provides training to volunteers, educational assistants, and older students who will be coaching EIR students as they read their EIR stories in a one-on-one situation.

See the DVD for full-size versions of all the forms in this chapter.

▶ To introduce EIR, first review the basic elements of the program, Figure 8-7.

▶ Next, describe coaching. Have participants review the following list in Figure 8-8.

One-on-One Coaching Training Agenda

1. Welcome and Introductions
2. What is EIR?
3. What is coaching?
4. Coaching Demonstration
5. Demonstrate Practice Coaching with a Volunteer
6. Participants Practice Coaching
7. Discuss Participants' Role in EIR
8. Tips
9. Follow-Up Sessions
10. Questions, Concerns, Thoughts

Figure 8-6 One-on-One Coaching Training Agenda

Basic Elements of EIR

▶ Twenty minutes of daily supplemental reading instruction to small groups of six or seven struggling readers

▶ Children receiving EIR participate in all of the regular reading instruction

▶ Three-day cycle reading and rereading a picture book and engaging in word-level activities and sentence writing related to the story

▶ Teacher concentrates on keeping children focused, on coaching them in their use of decoding and self-monitoring strategies, and on praising them for attempts at independence

▶ Teacher consistently monitors strategies as needed and helps children with reading and writing so they are successful

▶ Parent involvement

Figure 8-7 Basic Elements of EIR

- Explain that coaching is giving children prompts, encouraging them, praising them as they attempt to figure out words on their own. Students have been learning a number of different strategies to figure out unknown words as they come to them. The purpose of coaching is to help children to learn to depend on themselves so they become good, independent readers. Show Figure 8-9 for prompts the coaches can use as they are working with the children.

- To illustrate coaching, show the following video clips:

   Grade 1, Video 8: Teacher working with a group of grade 1 children in early December on a familiar story

   Grade 1, Video 9: Teacher working with a group of grade 1 children in early December on a new story.

- Conduct a coaching demonstration by modeling, with volunteer, and through partner practice. Model coaching by working through a story. Then, ask for a volunteer who will read another text as you coach. Finally, let people practice coaching with a partner by using a third text.

- In conclusion, return to Figure 8-8 to review the coach's role. Also look at Figure 8-10, which provides tips for working with children. Ask for questions, thoughts, or concerns. Schedule another session once the coaches have been working with children for four or five weeks.

Independent Coaching Role

- Work with one child at a time

- Classroom teacher gives you the summary or book to use

- Child has a copy of the book

- Assist child in reading the summary or book

- First graders track

- Reinforce strategies

- Give appropriate praise

Figure 8-8 Independent Coaching Role

Prompts for Teaching Children Decoding and Self-Monitoring Strategies

- Look at the beginning letter. Can you think of a word that starts with that letter/sound and makes sense? (Use only in the fall.)

- Can you reread that? Did that make sense?

- You did a great job of figuring out that word. How did you do it?

- I like the way you self-corrected. How did you do that?

- Let's look at that word again. You said . . . . Does that make sense (or look and sound right)?

Figure 8-9 Prompts for Teaching Children Decoding and Self-Monitoring Strategies

---

Tips for Working with Children

▶ Let the child do the work. Do as little as possible for them.

▶ Have your strategy sheet with you. Use the strategies consistently to foster independence.

▶ Have the child reread from the beginning of the sentence once pausing to work on a word.

▶ Praise the child for successful use of strategies.

▶ When a child uses a strategy correctly, use the phrase, *"That's what good readers do!"*

▶ When a child is struggling, refocusing their attention often works. Say, "Take another look at that word or try again."

Figure 8-10 Tips for Working with Children

Summary

I cannot stress enough the importance of both ongoing professional learning experiences and the training of one-on-one coaches. While many believe these two components are extras, I have found that teachers who engage in professional learning experiences with colleagues feel successful and in turn their students are successful readers. Additionally, the one-on-one coaching may logistically be difficult to schedule, but it is imperative for struggling readers to receive as many opportunities as possible to practice and master reading with this much needed guided support.

It is my hope that this book and the forthcoming companion books for kindergarten, second grade, third grade, and grades fourth–fifth will help you and your school meet your struggling readers' needs. Should you have additional questions, go to www.heinemann.com and search by title *Catching Readers* on the Heinemann website and look for additional resources. This intervention model is worth the time needed. When you understand and implement EIR in your classroom, you will feel tremendous pride in what your students will accomplish, especially knowing you were instrumental in showing them the way. Thank you for the important work you do with and for children.

Works Cited

Adams, M. J. 1990. *Beginning to Read: Thinking and Learning About Print.* Cambridge, MA: MIT Press.

Allington, R. L., and S. A. Walmsley, eds. 2007. *No Quick Fix: Rethinking Literacy Programs in America's Elementary Schools* (RTI ed.). New York: Teachers College Press.

Anderson, N. A. 2007. *What Should I Read Aloud?* Newark, DE: International Reading Association.

Au, K. H. 2006. *Multicultural Issues and Literacy Achievement.* Mahwah, NJ: Lawrence Erlbaum.

Baumann, J. F., and E. J. Kame'enui. 2004. *Vocabulary Instruction: Research to Practice.* New York: Guilford.

Bear, D. R., M. Invernizzi, S. Templeton, and F. Johnston. 2007. *Words Their Way: Word Study for Phonics, Vocabulary, and Spelling Instruction,* 4th ed. Upper Saddle River, NJ: Pearson/Merrill Prentice Hall.

Beck, I. L. 2006. *Making Sense of Phonics: The Hows and Whys.* New York: Guilford.

Beck, I. L., and M. G. McKeown. 2002. "Text Talk: Capturing the Benefit of Read-Aloud Experience for Young Children. *The Reading Teacher* 55 (1): 10–20.

Beck, I. L., M. G. McKeown, and L. Kucan. 2002. *Bringing Words to Life: Robust Vocabulary Instruction.* New York: Guilford.

Blachowicz, C., and P. Fisher. 2000. "Vocabulary Instruction." In *Handbook of Reading Research, Volume III*, eds. M. L. Kamil, P. B. Mosenthal, P. D. Pearson, and R. Barr. Mahwah, NJ: Lawrence Erlbaum.

_____. 2002. *Teaching Vocabulary in All Classrooms.* 2d ed. Upper Saddle River, NJ: Pearson/Merrill Prentice Hall.

Block, C., and M. Pressley, eds. 2002. *Comprehension Strategies: Research-Based Practices.* New York: Guilford.

Bohn, C. M., A. D. Roehrig, and M. Pressley. 2004. "The First Days of School in the Classrooms of Two More Effective and Four Less Effective Primary-Grades Teachers." *The Elementary School Journal* 104: 271–87.

Browne, A. 1989. *Things I Like.* New York: Random House.

Carnine, D. W., J. Silbert, E. J. Kame'nui, and S. G. Tarver. 2004. *Direct Instruction Reading,* 4th ed. Upper Saddle River, NJ: Pearson.

Chorzempa, B. F., and S. Graham. 2006. "Primary-Grade Teachers' Use of Within-Class Ability Grouping in Reading." *Journal of Educational Psychology* 98: 529–41.

Christensen, C. A., and J. A. Bowey. 2005. "The Efficacy of Orthographic Rime, Grapheme-Phoneme Correspondence, and Implicit Phonics Approaches to Teaching Decoding Skills." *Scientific Studies of Reading* 9: 327–49.

Clay, M. 1993. *Reading Recovery: A Guidebook for Teachers in Training.* Portsmouth, NH: Heinemann.

Connor, C. M., F. J. Morrison, and L. E. Katch. 2004. "Beyond the Reading Wars: Exploring the Effect of Child-Instruction Interactions on Growth in Early Reading." *Scientific Studies of Reading* 8: 305–36.

Consortium for Responsible School Change. 2005. *Description of Common Findings Across Multiple Studies on School Change in Reading.* Minneapolis: University of Minnesota, Minnesota Center for Reading Research.

Cunningham, P. M. 2009. *Phonics They Use: Words for Reading and Writing.* 5th ed. Boston: Pearson.

Cunningham, P. M., and D. R. Smith. 2008. *Beyond Retelling: Toward Higher Level Thinking and Big Ideas.* Newark, DE: International Reading Association.

Day, J. P., D. L. Spiegel, J. McLellan, and V.B. Brown. 2002. *Moving Forward with Literature Circles.* New York: Scholastic.

DiCamillo, K. 2003. *The Tale of Despereaux: Being the Story of a Mouse, a Princess, Some Soup, and a Spool of Thread.* Cambridge, MA: Candlewick Press.

Dolezal, S. E., L. M. Welsh, M. Pressley, and M.M. Vincent. 2003. "How Nine Third-Grade Teachers Motivate Student Academic Engagement." *Elementary School Journal* 103: 239–67.

Duke, N.K., and V.S. Bennett-Armistead. 2003. *Reading and Writing Informational Text in the Primary Grades: Research-Based Practices.* New York: Scholastic.

Edwards, P. A. 2004. *Children's Literacy Development: Making It Happen Through School, Family, and Community Involvement.* Boston: Pearson/Allyn & Bacon.

Foorman, B. R., C. Schatsneider, M. N. Eakin, J. M. Fletcher, L. C. Moats, and D.J. Francis. 2006. "The Impact of Instructional Practices in Grades 1 and 2 on Reading and Spelling Achievement in High Poverty Schools." *Contemporary Educational Psychology* 31: 1–29.

Foorman, B. R., and J. Torgesen. 2001. "Critical Elements of Classroom and Small-Group Instruction Promote Reading Success in All Children." *Learning Disabilities Research and Practice* 16: 203–12.

Fountas, I. C., and G. S. Pinnell. 1996. *Guided Reading: Good First Teaching for All Children.* Portsmouth, NH: Heinemann.

Fuchs, D., L. Fuchs, and S. Vaughn, Eds. 2008. *Response to Intervention: An Overview for Educators.* Newark, DE: International Reading Association.

Fuchs, L. S., D. Fuchs, M. K. Hosp, and J. R. Jenkins. 2001. "Oral Reading Fluency as an Indicator of Reading Competence: A Theoretical, Empirical, and Historical Analysis." *Scientific Studies of Reading* 5: 239–56.

Gaitan, C. D. 2006. *Building Culturally Responsive Classrooms: A Guide for K–6 Teachers.* Thousand Oaks, CA: Corwin.

Galda, L., and B. Cullinan. 2010. *Literature on the Child.* 7th ed. Belmont, CA: Thomson/Wadsworth.

Gaskins, I. W. 2004. *Success with Struggling Readers: The Benchmark School Approach.* New York: Guilford.

Gaskins, I. W., L. C. Ehri, C. Cress, C. O'Hara, and D. Donnelly. 1996. "Procedures for Word Learning: Making Discoveries About Words." *The Reading Teacher* 50: 312–27.

Graves, M. F. 2007. "Conceptual and Empirical Bases for Providing Struggling Readers with Multifaceted and Long-Term Vocabulary Instruction." In *Effective Instruction for Struggling Readers K–6,* edited by B. M. Taylor and J. E. Ysseldyke, 55–83. New York: Teachers College Press.

Guthrie, J. T., A. Wigfield, P. Barbosa, K. C. Perencevich, A. Taboada, M. H. Davis, et al. 2004. "Increasing Reading Comprehension and Engagement Through Concept-Oriented Reading Instruction." *Journal of Educational Psychology* 96: 403–23.

Guthrie, J. T., A. Wigfield, and C. VonSecker. 2000. "Effects of Integrated Instruction on Motivation and Strategy Use in Reading." *Journal of Educational Psychology* 92: 331–41.

Hamre, B. K., and R. C. Pianta. 2005. "Can Instructional and Emotional Support in the First-Grade Classroom Make a Difference for Children at Risk of School Failure?" *Child Development* 76 (5): 949–67.

Hasbrouck, J., and G. A. Tindal. 2006. "Oral Reading Fluency Norms: A Valuable Assessment Tool for Reading Teachers." *The Reading Teacher* 59 (7): 636–44.

Heffernan, L. 2004. *Critical Literacy and Writer's Workshop.* Newark, DE: International Reading Association.

Hiebert, E. H., and B. M. Taylor. 2000. "Beginning Reading Instruction: Research on Early Interventions." In *Handbook of Reading Research, Volume III,* edited by M. L. Kamil, P. B. Mosenthal, P. D. Pearson, and R. Barr, 455–482. Mahwah, NJ: Lawrence Erlbaum.

Hiebert, E. H., J. M. Colt, S. L. Catto, and E. C. Gury. 1992. "Reading and Writing of First-Grade Students in a Restructured Chapter I Program." *American Educational Research Journal* 29: 545–72.

Hutchins, P. 1968. *Rosie's Walk.* New York: Macmillan.

Johns, J. L., and R. L. Berglund. 2005. *Fluency Strategies and Assessments.* Dubuque, IA: Kendall-Hunt.

Juel, C., and C. Minden-Cupp. 2000. "Learning to Read Words: Linguistic Units and Instructional Strategies." *Reading Research Quarterly* 35: 458–92.

Kelley, M. J., and N. Clausen-Grace. 2007. *Comprehension Shouldn't Be Silent.* Newark, DE: International Reading Association.

Kletsien, S. B., and M. J. Dreher. 2005. *Informational Text in K–3 Classrooms: Helping Children Read and Write.* Newark, DE: International Reading Association.

Klingner, J. K., S. Vaughn, M. E. Arguelles, M. T. Hughes, and S. A. Leftwich. 2004. "Collaborative Strategic Reading: Real World Lessons from Classroom Teachers." *Remedial and Special Education* 25: 291–302.

Knapp, M. S. 1995. *Teaching for Meaning in High-Poverty Classrooms.* New York: Teachers College Press.

Kraus, R. 1974. *Herman the Helper.* New York: Windmill Books.

Krauss, Ruth. 1945. *The Carrot Seed.* New York: Harper and Row.

Kuhn, M. R., and S. A. Stahl. 2003. "Fluency: A Review of Developmental and Remedial Practices." *Journal of Educational Psychology* 95: 3–21.

Lapp, D., D. Fisher, and T. D. Wolsey. 2009. *Literacy Growth for Every Child: Differentiated Small-Group Instruction, K–6.* New York: Guilford.

Leslie, L., and J. Caldwell. 2006. *Qualitative Reading Inventory—4.* Boston: Pearson.

Lipson, M. L., J. H. Mosenthal, J. Mekkelsen, and B. Russ. 2004. "Building Knowledge and Fashioning Success One School at a Time." *The Reading Teacher* 57 (6): 534–42.

Manning, M., G. Morrison, and D. Camp. 2009. *Creating the Best Literacy Block Ever.* New York: Scholastic.

Mathes, P. G., C. A. Denton, J. M. Fletcher, J. L. Anthony, D. J. Francis, and C. Schatschneider. 2005. "The Effects of Theoretically Different Instruction and Student Characteristics on the Skills of Struggling Readers." *Reading Research Quarterly* 40: 148–82.

McCormick, C. E., R. N. Throneburg, and J. M. Smitley. 2002. *A Sound Start: Phonemic Awareness Lessons for Reading Success.* New York: Guilford.

McCormick, S. 2007. *Instructing Students Who Have Literacy Problems.* 5th ed. Upper Saddle River, NJ: Pearson.

McKenna, M., and S. Stahl. 2003. *Assessment for Reading Instruction.* New York: Guilford.

McKeown, M. G., I. L. Beck, and R. G. K. Blake. 2009. "Rethinking Reading Comprehension Instruction: A Comparison of Instruction for Strategies and Content Approaches." *Reading Research Quarterly* 44 (3): 218–53.

Morrow, L. M. 2003. *Organizing and Managing the Language Arts Block: A Professional Development Guide.* New York: Guilford.

National Reading Panel (NRP). 2000. *Teaching Children to Read: An Evidence-Based Assessment of the Scientific Research Literature on Reading and Its Implications for Reading Instruction.* Rockville, MD: National Institute for Child Health and Human Development, National Institutes of Health.

Resnick, L. B., and S. Hampton. 2009. *Reading and Writing Grade by Grade.* Revised Edition. Newark, DE: International Reading Association.

Oczkus, L. D. 2003. *Reciprocal Teaching at Work: Strategies for Improving Reading Comprehension.* Newark DE: International Reading Association.

Olness, R. 2007. *Using Literature to Enhance Content Area Instruction: A Guide for K–5 Teachers.* Newark, DE: International Reading Association.

Opitz, M. F., and J. L. Harding-DeKam. 2007. "Understanding and Teaching English-Language Learners." *The Reading Teacher* 60 (6): 590–593.

Paratore, J. R., and R. L. McCormack, eds. 2007. *Classroom Literacy Assessment: Making Sense of What Students Know and Do.* New York: Guilford.

Pikulski, J. 1994. "Preventing Reading Failure: A Review of Five Effective Programs." *The Reading Teacher* 48: 30–39.

Pinnell, G., M. Fried, and R. Eustice. 1990. "Reading Recovery: Learning How to Make a Difference." *The Reading Teacher* 90: 160–183.

Pressley, M. 2001. *Effective Beginning Reading Instruction*: Executive Summary and Paper Commissioned by the National Reading Conference. Chicago, IL: National Reading Conference.

———. 2006. *Reading Instruction That Works: The Case for Balanced Teaching.* 3d ed. New York: Guilford.

Pressley, M., L. Mohan, L. M. Raphael, and L. Fingeret. 2007. "How Does Bennett Woods Elementary School Produce Such High Reading and Writing Achievement?" *Journal of Educational Psychology* 99 (2): 221–40.

Pressley, M., S. E. Dolezal, L. M. Raphael, L. Mohan, A. D. Roehrig, and K. Bogner. 2003. *Motivating Primary-Grade Students.* New York: Guilford.

Raphael, T. E., K. Highfield, and K. H. Au. 2006. *QAR Now.* New York: Scholastic.

Raphael, T. E, L. S. Pardo, and K. Highfield. 2002. *Book Club: A Literature-Based Curriculum.* 2d ed. Lawrence, MA: Small Planet.

Rasinski, T. V. 2000. "Speed Does Matter in Reading." *The Reading Teacher* 54 (2): 146–151.

———. 2003. *The Fluent Reader: Oral Reading Strategies for Building Word Recognition, Fluency, and Comprehension.* New York: Scholastic.

Reyes, P., J. D. Scribner, and A. P. Scribner, eds. 1999. *Lessons from High-Performing Hispanic Schools.* New York: Teachers College.

Rog, L. J. 2001. *Early Literacy Instruction in Kindergarten.* Newark, DE: International Reading Association.

Routman, R. 2003. *Reading Essentials*. Portsmouth, NH: Heinemann.

———. 2008. *Teaching Essentials*. Portsmouth, NH: Heinemann.

Samuels, S. J., and A. Farstrup, eds. 2006. *What Research Has to Say About Fluency Instruction*, 3d ed. Newark, DE: International Reading Association.

Saunders, W. M., and C. Goldenberg. 1999. "Effects of Instructional Conversations and Literature Logs on Limited and Fluent English Proficient Students' Story Comprehension and Thematic Understanding." *The Elementary School Journal* 99: 279–301.

Serravallo, J. 2010. *Teaching Reading in Small Groups*. Portsmouth, NH: Heinemann.

Snow, C. E., M. S. Burns, and P. Griffin, eds. 1998. *Preventing Reading Difficulties in Young Children*. Washington, DC: National Academy.

Southall, M. 2009. *Differentiated Small-Group Reading Lessons*. New York: Scholastic.

Stahl, S. A. 2001. "Teaching Phonics and Phonemic Awareness." In *Handbook of Early Literacy Research* (333–347), edited by S. B. Neuman and D. Dickenson. New York: Guilford.

Stahl, S. A., and M. R. Kuhn. 2002. "Making It Sound Like Language: Developing Fluency." *The Reading Teacher* 55 (6): 582–584.

Taberski, S. 2000. *On Solid Ground: Strategies for Teaching Reading K–3*. Portsmouth, NH: Heinemann.

Taylor, B. M. 1991. "A Test of Phonemic Awareness for Classroom Use." www.earlyinterventioninreading.com.

———. 1998. "A Brief Review of Research on the Learning to Read Process." Minneapolis: University of Minnesota.

———. 2001. *The Early Intervention in Reading Program: Research and Development Spanning Twelve Years*. www.earlyinterventioninreading.com.

———. 2010a. *Catching Readers, Grade 2*. Portsmouth, NH: Heinemann.

———. 2010b. *Catching Readers, Grade 3*. Portsmouth, NH: Heinemann.

———. 2010c. *Developing Successful Engaged Readers, K–8: A School-Based Professional Learning Model That Works*. Portsmouth, NH: Heinemann.

Taylor, B. M., B. Hanson, K. J. Justice-Swanson, and S. Watts. 1997. "Helping Struggling Readers: Linking Small Group Intervention with Cross-Age Tutoring." *The Reading Teacher* 51: 196–209.

Taylor, B. M., L. Harris, P. D. Pearson, and G. E. Garcia. 1995. *Reading Difficulties: Instruction and Assessment*, 2d ed. New York: Random House.

Taylor, B. M., and P. D. Pearson, eds. 2002. *Teaching Reading: Effective Schools/Accomplished Teachers*. Mahwah, NJ: Erlbaum.

Taylor, B. M., P. D. Pearson, K. Clark, and S. Walpole. 2000. "Effective Schools and Accomplished Teachers: Lessons About Primary Grade Reading Instruction in Low-Income Schools." *Elementary School Journal* 101 (2): 121–66.

Taylor, B. M., P. D. Pearson, D. S. Peterson, and M. C. Rodriguez. 2003. "Reading Growth in High-Poverty Classrooms: The Influence of Teacher Practices That Encourage Cognitive Engagement in Literacy Learning." *Elementary School Journal* 104: 3–28.

Taylor, B. M., P. D. Pearson, D. S. Peterson, and M. C. Rodriguez. 2005. "The CIERA School Change Framework: An Evidence-Based Approach to Professional Development and School Reading Improvement." *Reading Research Quarterly* 40 (1): 40–69.

Taylor, B. M., D. S. Peterson, M. Marx, and M. Chein. 2007. "Scaling Up a Reading Reform in High-Poverty Elementary Schools." In *Effective Instruction for Struggling Readers, K–6*, edited by B. M. Taylor and J. E. Ysseldyke. New York: Teachers College Press.

Taylor, B. M., D.S. Peterson, P.D. Pearson, and M.C. Rodriguez. 2002. "Looking Inside Classrooms: Reflecting on the 'How' as Well as the 'What' in Effective Reading Instruction." *The Reading Teacher* 56: 70–79.

Taylor, B. M., M. Pressley, and P.D. Pearson. 2002. "Research-Supported Characteristics of Teachers and Schools That Promote Reading Achievement." In *Teaching Reading: Effective Schools, Accomplished Teachers*, edited by B. M. Taylor and P. D. Pearson. Mahwah, NJ: Lawrence Erlbaum, 36–74.

Taylor, B. M., Raphael, T. E., and Au, K.H. (in press). "Reading and School Reform." In *Handbook of Reading Research, volume 4*, edited by M. Kamil, P. D. Pearson, P. Afflerbach, and E. Moje. London: Taylor & Francis.

Taylor, B. M., R. Short, B. Frye, and B. Shearer. 1992. "Classroom Teachers Prevent Reading Failure Among Low-Achieving First-Grade Students." *The Reading Teacher* 45: 592–97.

Valli, L., R.G. Croninger, and K. Walters. 2007. "Who (Else) Is the Teacher? Cautionary Notes on Teacher Accountability Systems." *American Journal of Education* 113: 635–62.

Vaughn, S., J. Wanzek, and J. M. Fletcher. 2007. "Multiple Tiers of Intervention: A Framework for Prevention and Identification of Students with Reading/Learning Disabilities." In *Effective Instruction for Struggling Readers K–6*, edited by B. M. Taylor and J. E. Ysseldyke, 173–195. New York: Teachers College Press.

Van den Branden, K. 2000. "Does Negotiation of Meaning Promote Reading Comprehension? A Study of Multilingual Primary School Classes." *Reading Research Quarterly* 35: 426–43.

Walpole, S., and M. C. McKenna. 2009. *How to Plan Differentiated Reading Instruction: Resources for Grades K–3.* New York: Guilford.

Wood, K. D., N. L. Roser, and M. Martinez. 2001. "Collaborative Literacy: Lessons Learned from Literature." *The Reading Teacher* 55 (2): 102–111.

Recommended Professional Readings

Resources on Phonemic Awareness

McCormick, C. E., R. N. Throneburg, and J. M. Smitley. 2002. *A Sound Start: Phonemic Awareness Lessons for Reading Success.* New York: Guilford.

Rog, L. J. 2001. *Early Literacy Instruction in Kindergarten.* Newark, DE: International Reading Association.

Resources on Phonics and Word Recognition Instruction

Bear, D. R., M. Invernizzi, S. Templeton, and F. Johnston. 2007. *Words Their Way: Word Study for Phonics, Vocabulary, and Spelling Instruction*, 4th ed. Upper Saddle River, NJ: Pearson/Merrill Prentice Hall.

Beck, I. 2006. *Making Sense of Phonics: The Hows and Whys.* New York: Guilford.

Cunningham, P. 2009. *Phonics They Use: Words for Reading and Writing,* 5th ed. Boston: Pearson.

Carnine, D. W., J. Silbert, E.J. Kame'enui, and S. G. Tarver. 2004. *Direct Instruction Reading*, 4th ed. Upper Saddle River, NJ: Pearson.

Gaskins, I. W., L. C. Ehri, C. Cress, C. O'Hara, and D. Donnelly. 1996. "Procedures for Word Learning: Making Discoveries About Words." *The Reading Teacher*, (50): 312–27.

Taylor, B., R. Short, B. Frye, and B. Shearer. 1992. "Classroom Teachers Prevent Reading Failure Among Low-Achieving First-Grade Students." *The Reading Teacher* (45): 592–97.

Resources on Fluency

Johns, J. L., and R. L. Berglund. 2005. *Fluency Strategies and Assessments.* Dubuque, IA: Kendall-Hunt.

Rasinski, T. V. 2003. *The Fluent Reader: Oral Reading Strategies for Building Word Recognition, Fluency, and Comprehension.* New York: Scholastic.

———. 2000. "Speed Does Matter in Reading." *The Reading Teacher* 54 (2): 146–51.

Samuels, S. J., and A. Farstrup, eds. 2006. *What Research Has to Say About Fluency Instruction*, 3d ed. Newark, DE: International Reading Association.

Stahl, S. A., and M. R. Kuhn. 2002. "Making It Sound Like Language: Developing Fluency." *The Reading Teacher* 55 (6): 582–584.

Resources on Vocabulary:

Bauman, J. F., and E. J. Kame'enui, eds., 2004. *Vocabulary Instruction: Research to Practice.* New York: Guilford.

Beck, I. L., and M. G. McKeown. 2002. "Text Talk: Capturing the Benefit of Read-Aloud Experience for Young Children." *Reading Teacher* 55 (1): 10–20.

Beck, I., M. McKeown, and L. Kucan. 2002. *Bringing Words to Life: Robust Vocabulary Instruction.* New York: Guilford.

Blachowicz, C., and P. Fisher. 2002. *Teaching Vocabulary in All Classrooms*, 2d ed. Upper Saddle River, NJ: Pearson/Merrill Prentice Hall.

Graves, M. F. 2007. "Conceptual and Empirical Bases for Providing Struggling Readers with Multifaceted and Long-Term Vocabulary Instruction." In *Effective Instruction for Struggling Readers K–6*, edited by B. M. Taylor and J. E. Ysseldyke, 55–83. New York: Teachers College Press.

Resources on Comprehension Strategies

Block, C., and M. Pressley, eds. 2002. *Comprehension Strategies: Research-based Practices.* New York: Guilford.

Duke, N. K., and V. S. Bennett-Armistead. 2003. *Reading and Writing Informational Text in the Primary Grades.* New York: Scholastic.

Kelley, M. J., and N. Clausen-Grace. 2007. *Comprehension Shouldn't Be Silent.* Newark, DE: International Reading Association.

Kletsien, S. B, and M. J. Dreher. 2005. *Informational Text in K–3 Classrooms: Helping Children Read and Write.* Newark, DE: International Reading Association.

Klingner, J. K., S. Vaughan, M. E. Arguelles, M. T. Hughes, and S. A. Leftwich. 2004. "Collaborative Strategic Reading: Real World Lessons from Classroom Teachers." *Remedial and Special Education* (25): 291–302

Raphael, T. E., K. Highfield, and K. H. Au. 2006. *QAR Now.* New York: Scholastic.

Resources on Comprehension: High-Level Talk and Writing About Text

Anderson, N. A. 2007. *What Should I Read Aloud?* Newark, DE: International Reading Association.

Beck, I. L., and M. G. McKeown. 2002. "Text Talk: Capturing the Benefit of Read-Aloud Experience for Young Children." *The Reading Teacher* 55 (1): 10–20.

Cunningham, P. M., and D. R. Smith. 2008. *Beyond Retelling: Toward Higher Level Thinking and Big Ideas.* Newark DE: International Reading Association.

Day, J. P., D. L. Spiegel, J. McLellan, and V. B. Brown. 2002. *Moving Forward with Literature Circles.* New York: Scholastic.

Galda, L., and B. Cullinan. 2010. *Literature on the Child,* Seventh edition. Belmont, CA: Thomson/Wadsworth.

Kelley, M. J., and N. Clausen-Grace. 2007. *Comprehension Shouldn't Be Silent.* Newark, DE: International Reading Association.

Olness, R. 2007. *Using Literature to Enhance Content Area Instruction: A Guide for K–5 Teachers.* Newark, DE: International Reading Association.

Raphael, T. E, L. S. Pardo, and L. Highfield. 2002. *Book Club: A Literature-Based Curriculum.* 2d ed. Lawrence, MA: Small Planet.

Raphael, T. R., and S. McMahon. 1994. "Book Club: An Alternative Framework for Reading Instruction." *The Reading Teacher* 48 (2): 102–116.

Wood, K. D., N. L. Roser, and M. Martinez, M. 2001. "Collaborative Literacy: Lessons Learned from Literature." *The Reading Teacher* 55 (2): 102–111.

Resources on Balanced, Differentiated Instruction

Fountas, I. C., and G. S. Pinnell. 1996. *Guided Reading: Good First Teaching for All Children.* Portsmouth, NH: Heinemann.

Lapp, D., D. Fisher, and T. D. Wolsey. 2009. *Literacy Growth for Every Child: Differentiated Small-Group Instruction, K–6.* New York: Guilford.

Manning, M., G. Morrison, and D. Camp. 2009. *Creating the Best Literacy Block Ever.* New York: Scholastic.

Morrow, L. M. 2003. *Organizing and Managing the Language Arts Block: A Professional Development Guide.* New York: Guilford.

Pressley, M. 2006. *Reading Instruction That Works: The Case for Balanced Teaching,* 3d ed. New York: Guilford.

Routman, R. 2003. *Reading Essentials: The Specifics You Need to Teach Reading Well.* Portsmouth, NH: Heinemann.

———. 2008. *Teaching Essentials: Expecting the Most and Getting the Best from Every Learner, K–8.* Portsmouth, NH: Heinemann.

Serravallo, J. 2009. *Reading Instruction in Small Groups.* Portsmouth, NH: Heinemann.

Southall, M. 2009. *Differentiated Small-Group Reading Lessons.* New York: Scholastic.

Taberski, S. 2000. *On Solid Ground: Strategies for Teaching Reading K–3.* Portsmouth, NH: Heinemann.

Walpole, S., and M. C. McKenna. 2009. *How to Plan Differentiated Reading Instruction: Resources for Grades K–3.* New York: Guilford.

Resources on Support for Struggling Readers

Fuchs, D., L. Fuchs, and S. Vaughn, eds. 2008. *Response to Intervention: An Overview for Educators.* Newark, DE: International Reading Association.

Gaskins, I. W. 2004. *Success with Struggling Readers: The Benchmark School Approach.* New York: Guilford.

McCormick, S. 2007. *Instructing Students Who Have Literacy Problems,* 5th ed. Upper Saddle River, NJ: Pearson.

Taylor, B. M. 2010a. *Catching Readers, Grade 2.* Portsmouth, NH: Heinemann.

———. 2010b. *Catching Readers, Grade 3.* Portsmouth, NH: Heinemann.

Tyner, B. 2009. *Small-Group Reading Instruction: A Differentiated Teaching Model for Beginning and Struggling Readers.* Newark, DE: International Reading Association.

Tyner, B., and S. E. Green. 2005. *Small-Group Reading Instruction: A Differentiated Teaching Model for Intermediate Grade Readers, Grades 3–8.* Newark, DE: International Reading Association.

Vaughn, S., J. Wanzek, and J. M. Fletcher. 2007. "Multiple Tiers of Intervention: A Framework for Prevention and Identification of Students with Reading/Learning Disabilities." In *Effective Instruction for Struggling Readers K–6,* edited by B. M. Taylor and J. E. Ysseldyke, 173–195. New York: Teachers College Press.

Resources on Motivating, Effective Pedagogy

Connor, C. M., F. J. Morrison, and L. E. Katch. 2004. "Beyond the Reading Wars: Exploring the Effect of Child-Instruction Interactions on Growth in Early Reading." *Scientific Studies of Reading* (8): 305–36.

Kelley, M. J., and N. Clausen-Grace. 2007. *Comprehension Shouldn't Be Silent.* Newark, DE: International Reading Association.

Manning, M., G. Morrison, and D. Camp. 2009. *Creating the Best Literacy Block Ever.* New York: Scholastic.

Olness, R. 2007. *Using Literature to Enhance Content-Area Instruction: A Guide for K–5 Teachers.* Newark, DE: International Reading Association.

Pressley, M. 2006. *Reading Instruction That Works: The Case for Balanced Teaching,* Third edition. New York: Guilford.

Pressley, M., S. E. Dolezal, L. M. Raphael, L. Mohan, L., A. D. Roehrig, and K. Bogner. 2003. *Motivating Primary-Grade Students.* New York: Guilford.

Resources on Assessments

McKenna, M., and S. Stahl, S. 2003. *Assessment for Reading Instruction.* New York: Guilford.

Paratore, J. R., and R. L. McCormick, eds. 2007. *Classroom Reading Assessment: Making Sense of What Students Know and Do.* New York: Guilford.

Pressley, M. 2006. *Reading Instruction That Works: The Case for Balanced Teaching,* 3d ed. New York: Guilford.

Taberski, S. 2000. *On Solid Ground: Strategies for Teaching Reading K–3.* Portsmouth, NH: Heinemann.

Resources on Culturally Responsive Instruction

Au, K. 2006. *Multicultural Issues and Literacy Achievement.* Mahwah, NJ: Erlbaum.

Gaitan, C. D. 2006. *Building Culturally Responsive Classrooms: A Guide for K–6 Teachers.* Thousand Oaks, CA: Corwin.

For a list and review of books for teachers on English language learners, see Opitz, M. F., and J. L. Harding-DeKam. 2007. "Teaching English-Language Learners." *The Reading Teacher* 60 (6): 590–93.

Resources on Schoolwide Reading Programs and Effective Schools

Allington, R. L., and S. A. Walmsley, eds. 2007. *No Quick Fix: Rethinking Literacy Programs in American's Elementary Schools* (RTI ed.). New York: Teachers College Press.

Morrow, L. M. 2003. *Organizing and Managing the Language Arts Block: A Professional Development Guide.* New York: Guilford.

New Standards Primary Literacy Committee. 1999. *Reading and Writing Grade by Grade.* Washington, DC: National Center on Education and the Economy (NCEE).

Reyes, P., J. D. Scribner, and A. P. Scribner, eds. 1999. *Lessons from High-Performing Hispanic Schools.* New York: Teachers College Press.

Taylor, B. M., P. D. Pearson, eds. 2002. *Teaching Reading: Effective Schools/Accomplished Teachers.* Mahwah, NJ: Erlbaum.

Taylor, B. M., D. S. Peterson, M. Marx, and M. Chein. 2007. "Scaling Up a Reading Framework for Prevention and Identification of Students with Reading/Learning Disabilities." In *Effective Instruction for Struggling Readers K–6,* edited by B. M. Taylor and J. E. Ysseldyke, 216–234. New York: Teachers College Press.

Taylor, B. M. 2010c. *Developing Successful, Engaged Readers, K–8: A School-Based Professional Learning Model That Works.* Portsmouth, NH: Heinemann.